BRADGATE PARK
Childhood Home of Lady Jane Grey
Joan Stevenson
Anthony Squires

Second Edition:
Fully revised and expanded

KAIROS PRESS
Newtown Linford
Leicestershire
1999

ISBN 1 871344 23 9

First edition (ISBN 1-971344-02-6) 1994
Second edition, 1999

Design and layout by Robin Stevenson, Kairos Press.
Body text in Aldine 721 BT 10.5 pt.
Imagesetting by Qualitype, Leicester.
Printed in Great Britain by Norwood Press, Anstey, Leicester.

British Library Cataloguing in Publication Data.
A catalogue record for this book is available from the British Library.

KAIROS PRESS
552 Bradgate Road
Newtown Linford
Leicestershire, LE6 0HB

Front cover: Exploring around the ruins of Bradgate House.

CONTENTS

4

List of Illustrations

Maps, Diagrams, and Feature Boxes

1. BRADGATE: A MEDIEVAL DEER PARK

*W*hen William the Conquerer came to England in 1066, he handed over large tracts of the country to his friends. Hugh de Grentmesnil, who was granted much of Leicestershire, was lucky to survive the Battle of Hastings. His horse broke its bridle rein while leaping over a bush and bolted towards the enemy. The sight of English defenders charging forwards with raised hatchets, though, caused it to turn about and bolt back to safety. Among the lands given to Hugh was the Manor of Groby, including the area now known as Bradgate Park.

Bradgate was part of the waste of Charnwood Forest. There were the same rocky outcrops we know today, more trees, heather and gorse, but less bracken. There were red and roe deer and big birds of prey such as buzzards, peregrines and eagles, but no fallow deer, no rabbits and no rats. There was no village of Newtown Linford and no tillage, just rough grazing. Indeed there was no village between Anstey and Shepshed, except, maybe, small pioneer Scandinavian settlements at Charley and Ulverscroft.

Groby Manor stretched from Botcheston, Newtown Unthank and Ratby in the south to Swithland in the east, encompassing Ulverscroft and Bradgate. This area of Leicestershire held no particular interest to Hugh, and he may not even have visited it.

Bradgate Park and the Manor of Groby

The medieval manor of Groby, on the southern fringe of Charnwood Forest, extended from Botcheston, Newtown Unthank, Ratby and Groby (seen lower left in the picture above) in the south and west, over the Forest to Swithland (far distance right) in the north-east. From the mid thirteenth century the manor was owned by the Ferrers family who lived in a house on the site of the present Groby Old Hall. In the mid fifteenth century it passed by marriage to the Greys. The villages of Newtown Linford (middle left) and Bradgate (now lost, see page 14), existed as poor settlements in the waste of Charnwood with the original hunting park of the Ferrers occupying particularly rocky and infertile ground (upper centre). The present park was begun by Thomas Grey (1451-1501) and completed by his son Thomas (1477-1530). Groby Pool, noted in medieval times for the value of its fishing, can be seen at the bottom right of the aerial photograph above.

Rocks in Bradgate

Bradgate contains some of the oldest and hardest rocks in Britain, and is an area of particular interest to geologists. Some of the rocks formed deep underground, as molten material which cooled and crystallized to make granites. Others began in water, as layers of sediment, still others from the settling dust and ash errupted from a volcano. The layers of sediment were later compressed into slaty rocks. What was once a high mountain range over Charnwood has eroded, exposing craggy cliffs.

Bradgate's granite is very hard, and occurs as massive blocks of stone. Examined closely, a mass of crystals can be seen, showing that it slowly solidified from molten magma deep underground. It forms the cliffs along the Little Matlock gorge, to Bradgate House, and continues up the hill as far as Tyburn and Bowling Green Plantation.

All the other stone is made up of various sorts of sedimentary rocks. Most of these are formed by layers of sand, silt or clay building up and cementing together under water. They all show something of their original layered forms, but have been subsequently changed by the effects of heat and pressure because of being buried deep underground. Their present appearance is affected both by the nature of that pressure (which has caused some layers to be twisted and folded) and the nature of the original materials. Some, such as the Swithland slates, started as fine muds which eventually became the smooth slabs used for house roofs. Swithland slate is best seen in the neighbouring

Above: The large granite blocks of the Little Matlock gorge.

Swithland Woods, but it also occurs between the Deer Barn and Hallgates.

Some of the most dramatic and geologically interesting rocks can be found just south of Old John. A line of craggy cliffs runs between the War Memorial and Sliding Stone Spinney. These are known as Slump Breccia, and formed as a mixture of muds and ash from Charnwood's volcano. They now appear as very brittle, sharply fractured rocks, containing faint traces of some of the earliest fossil marks in Britain, so do not damage these, or any other of the rocks at Bradgate.

South of these cliffs, the rock is a softer sedimentary material known as Bradgate Tuff Formation, producing a more rounded landscape. North of the

the accumulation of wind-blown dust in shallow lakes and pools. A particularly striking example of this clay is the red 'cliff' exposed on the south bank of the River Lyn, not far from Bradgate House.

On top of all these rocks, the most recent deposits are from the melting ice sheets of the last Ice Age. As the huge glacial sheet melted it left behind clay, sand, pebbles, even boulders, which had travelled in the ice from all over Northern Britain. The result is known as Boulder Clay. So in amongst the 'bedrock' stones you may also find all sorts of rocks which don't really 'belong' here. Another effect of the glaciation was probably to divert a big torrent of meltwater down a previously small valley, which then became the spectacular gorge at Little Matlock.

Above: Slump Breccia – ancient brittle rocks made from volcanic ash, south of the War Memorial.

Right: Swithland slates outcrop near the Hallgates entrance, overlooking Cropston Reservoir

slump breccia are other sedimentary rocks, the Beacon Hill Tuff Formation, and these form the dramatic hill top of Old John.

In places, layers of red clay lie on top of these ancient hard rocks. These are known as Mercian Mudstones, and were formed in desert conditions from

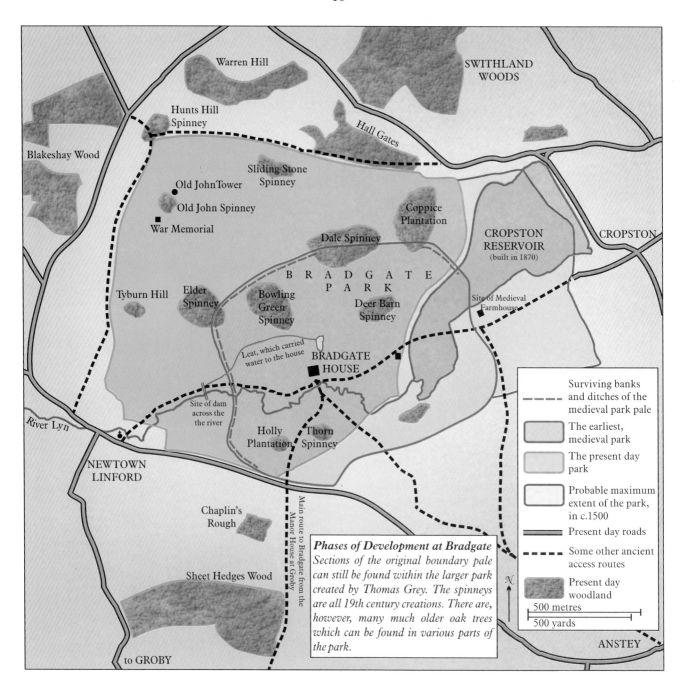

Warren Hill

SWITHLAND WOODS

Hunts Hill Spinney

Hall Gates

Blakeshay Wood

Sliding Stone Spinney

Old John Tower

Old John Spinney

Coppice Plantation

War Memorial

Dale Spinney

CROPSTON RESERVOIR (built in 1870)

CROPSTON

B R A D G A T E P A R K

Tyburn Hill

Elder Spinney

Bowling Green Spinney

Deer Barn Spinney

Site of Medieval Farmhouse

Leat, which carried water to the house

BRADGATE HOUSE

River Lyn

Site of dam across the the river

Holly Plantation

Thorn Spinney

NEWTOWN LINFORD

Chaplin's Rough

Main route to Bradgate from the Manor House at Groby

Phases of Development at Bradgate
Sections of the original boundary pale can still be found within the larger park created by Thomas Grey. The spinneys are all 19th century creations. There are, however, many much older oak trees which can be found in various parts of the park.

Sheet Hedges Wood

N

to GROBY

ANSTEY

Surviving banks and ditches of the medieval park pale

The earliest, medieval park

The present day park

Probable maximum extent of the park, in c.1500

Present day roads

Some other ancient access routes

Present day woodland

500 metres
500 yards

After Hugh's time, Groby had a number of different owners, and was one of several such Manors — including Barrow, Shepshed, Whitwick and Belton — which encircled Charnwood Forest. All the manors included at least one deer park. Groby had two: Groby Park and Bradgate Park.

There were hundreds of deer parks in England in the middle ages, including about fifty in Leicestershire, and a large landowner might have one or more parks in each of his various manors. Bradgate Park is a rare relic of the days when an ostentatiously rich baron could enjoy hunting his deer and also show the world that he was a person of wealth and property.

Because of its rocky outcrops and steep gradients, Bradgate was never very suitable for agriculture, so stocking it with deer was a sensible use of the land. Although nowadays we see Bradgate Park as a more or less wild and natural landscape encircled by pastures

and fields under cultivation, in earlier days it was the park which was more carefully tended than the surrounding forest. It was looked after by parkers, whose job it was to ensure that there were always deer when they were needed for food or sport.

The first recorded mention of Bradgate Park is dated 1241, when the earl of Winchester was given the right to take deer with nine bows and six hounds. Bradgate may have been established well before then. Its present boundaries, though, are not the same as those of the thirteenth century. When a medieval park was being planned, careful account was taken of the rise and fall of the landscape. One of the most important and difficult tasks of the parkers was to stop the deer escaping. Boundaries were marked not by stone walls, as at present, but by an internal ditch and an outer bank topped by a wooden fence, the whole being known as a pale. Ideally, the pale would run across a rising hillside

The parker's house was surrounded by a moat. It was probably never designed to be permanently filled with water, but would have become so in wet periods. As this picture shows, it still does.

so that the deer, running uphill, would find it much harder to jump out. To keep the expensive perimeter pale as short as possible, and keep as much of the pale as possible on rising ground, the optimum shape for a deer park was that of a saucer.

The present Bradgate boundaries, however, do not make sense from the viewpoint of a medieval surveyor. The park is square rather than round, which is wasteful of fencing, and some of its perimeter walls are on falling ground. The discovery of remains of boundary ditches within the park shows that there was an earlier, considerably smaller Bradgate Park. This was the hunting ground of medieval lords of Groby until the whole area was redeveloped at the end of the fifteenth century.

Deer were a valuable commodity, and folk from the nearby villages would have welcomed the chance to cook some stolen venison (and probably did, from time to time). Being a parker was potentially a dangerous job — not because of the animals, but because of the poachers. At Bradgate, as at other parks, the parker lived in a house surrounded by a small moat, which at least reduced the chance of his being murdered in his bed. The house at Bradgate, which would have been of timber construction, is long gone, but the moated site is still visible, and the moat still fills with water in a wet season. It is close to the main drive between the greensward and the ruins, close to a solitary conifer which stands on a small mound. (see item 9 on the self guided walk, pages 77-79).

There used to be a village of Bradgate, which was quite separate from that of Newtown Linford. It is one of the least known of the many lost villages of Leicestershire, and its position has always been something of a puzzle. The sites of two houses are known, and it appears to have been a small, dispersed settlement rather than a nucleated village. It would have been easy to destroy during the big changes which accompanied the building of Bradgate House around 1500. Thomas Grey was in fact summoned for depopulation, but claimed that he had rehoused the inhabitants elsewhere.

2. THE RISE OF THE GREYS

*F*rom 1279 till 1445 Groby Manor was owned by the Ferrers family, and passed into the hands of the Greys by marriage. Edward, younger son of lord Reginald Grey, third baron Grey of Ruthin, married heiress Elizabeth Ferrers in 1427, and was himself created lord Ferrers and baron Grey of Groby after the death of Elizabeth's grandfather in 1445. Their son, Sir John Grey, changed the family fortunes for all time when he married Elizabeth Woodville of Grafton in Northamptonshire. It was a spectacularly good marriage for him. Elizabeth's mother was a minor European

princess, Jacquetta of Luxemburg, whose first husband had been the elderly duke of Bedford, brother of King Henry V. After the duke's death Jacquetta married the man of her own choice, Sir Richard Woodville. They had five sons and seven daughters, of whom Elizabeth was the eldest.

Elizabeth was about fifteen when she married Sir John Grey, on the eve of the civil strife known as the Wars of the Roses. Two sons, Thomas and Richard, were born; but then Sir John, a Lancastrian, was killed at the second Battle of St Albans in 1461 and the Grey estates were confiscated. Elizabeth, widowed and homeless, took her children back to her parents' house in Northamptonshire.

Desperate to retrieve her husband's inheritance for her sons, Elizabeth waylaid the king, the Yorkist Edward IV, as he hunted in the forest near Grafton. From this meeting there ensued a romance which culminated in a secret wedding. When Edward was compelled to admit to the marriage, there was an outcry from nobles and people alike, for the marriage of a king was supposed to be a matter of high diplomacy, not personal attachment. The deed was done, however, and Dame Elizabeth Grey became Queen of England.

Elizabeth's life from then on was far from smooth; she spent periods in sanctuary, and her son, Edward, heir to his father's throne, was born in Westminster Abbey during one such episode. The greatest tragedy of Elizabeth's life followed the death of her husband. Instead of her son being crowned Edward V, his uncle Richard seized the throne to become Richard III, and Edward and his brother Richard disappeared, becoming

Groby Manor was the Grey family home until Bradgate House was built in the early sixteenth century.

The Village of Bradgate

Nothing now remains of the former village of Bradgate. It was never more than a small settlement and is first mentioned by name in 1377, when 41 persons contributed to the notorious poll tax of that year. A second assessment of a similar nature, made before 1400, mentions 29 tax payers from the village. When the first marquess of Dorset began work on the building of Bradgate House at the end of the 15th century, he swept away all the dwellings in order to enlarge the park. For this act of depopulation, a serious crime at the time, he was summoned to answer in Chancery. There he pleaded he had re-housed the villagers elsewhere. When hearths were taxed in 1670, only Bradgate House remained. In 1801 there were 8 persons in Bradgate Park, and in 1871 a total of 12. Subsequent totals were included in the returns for Newtown.

Local historian David Ramsey has brought together documentary and archaeological evidence to show where the 14th century village of Bradgate was located. He has also indicated that the village was re-located not once, but twice, by the Greys. The first Bradgate was a small scattered group of dwellings in the waste of Groby and lay to the north east of the ancient hunting park of the Ferrers. The lands of the village extended south to the 'Broadgate' – a wide road known today as Causeway Lane, Cropston. When Thomas Grey extended the boundary of the ancient park to create his new park about the year 1500, the villagers were moved to a site to the south of the Broadgate. Finally, between 1562 and 1600, the villagers were encouraged to move yet again, this time to near the present Coach and Horses public house at Field Head.

The emptying of the reservoir in 1988 revealed ridge and furrow ploughland of the first village (bottom right) as well as a section of the ancient deer park pale (the middle one of three lines seen running across the reservoir floor). The site of at least one of the houses has been discovered in a field near the edge of the reservoir. It shows as a mark in the soil, which can be seen half way up the field on the left of the photograph. Although it was badly damaged by ploughing during World War Two the evidence produced a ground plan of a building which indicated a large rectangular ditched site with internal subdivisions. Pottery fragments from the thirteenth to seventeenth centuries have also been found. A second pottery scatter has been located in the area of the Hallgates car park.

known to posterity as the Princes in the Tower – believed to have beeen smothered at the instigation of their uncle.

The Battle of Bosworth Field in 1485, only a few miles from Bradgate, brought another change in Elizabeth's fortunes. The death, during the battle, of Richard III led to the accession of Henry VII, who kept his promise to unite the houses of York and Lancaster by marrying Elizabeth of York, daughter of Elizabeth Woodville and Edward IV.

Elizabeth's two children by her first marriage were brought up as stepsons of the king of England, and became embroiled in the problems of the succession to the throne. As a result, the younger brother, Richard Grey, lost his head — an occupational hazard for members of conspicuous families.

A section of the pale of the original park of the Ferrers, seen here as it passes through Elder Spinney. A park pale consisted of a ditch with an external bank topped with a wooden fence, in order to prevent the deer from escaping. The spinneys were planted in the 19th century. However, inside the park, many ancient oaks remain, some perhaps dating from this earlier phase of the park's history.

Overleaf: The park pale is shown very clearly where the River Lyn has cut away a section to reveal its profile. This area, just downstream from Little Matlock gorge, shows the bank (on the right) with the ditch to the left. The area on the right of the photograph would have been outside the medieval park. A line of ancient oak trees can be seen growing along the pale where it runs through the deer sanctuary on the far bank.

3. THE BUILDING OF BRADGATE HOUSE

*E*lizabeth's eldest son, Thomas, survived the wars, and was created marquess of Dorset. Whenever he could he turned to his country estates and threw his considerable energies into improving his various properties. At Groby he began to modernise the manor house, probably between 1488 and 1492. It was hopelessly old fashioned, in need of much repair and no longer suitable for a man of his status. The Tudor scholar and traveller John Leland (1506-1552) noted how he had begun 'foundations and walls of a great house' at Groby, but had left them half finished (see page 27).

At a late stage in the modernisation of Groby, Thomas Grey abruptly abandoned the work and embarked on a much more ambitious project: the enlargement of the old hunting park of his Ferrers ancestors and the building of a great new mansion there. Sadly, all that remain today are the romantic ruins of the principle rooms and towers, all long decayed and plundered and open to the sky, together with their grounds and gardens in the styles and designs of the 16th and 17th centuries.

It is not difficult to understand why the first marquess undertook such an ambitious scheme. He was, after all, related by marriage to King Henry VII and frequented the royal court. Here was a jungle of great social and political rivalry, where men jockeyed for royal favour and the fruits of high office. Under the king, victor of Bosworth Field in 1485, the old ideas of the middle ages were clearly set to change. The lord's castle and the gentleman's fortified manor house, built in times of great unrest, were quickly destined to become dwellings of the past. All around men of rank and substance were beginning to express themselves in new ways on the landscape by erecting large houses set in new style parks. It was important Thomas moved with the times, not just following others but leading the field.

Yet his relationship with the king produced problems for the Greys. Not without good reasons, Henry VII continued to have grave doubts about their loyalty. He once sent the marquess to prison and obliged the man to lodge large sums of money against his continued good behaviour. By the time of his death in 1501 the marquess had probably had little opportunity to make much headway with his plans for Bradgate. It was left to his son Thomas, the 2nd marquess to construct the mansion.

The second Thomas's relationship with Henry VII was also troubled and he too spent time in the Tower and, in addition, an extended exile in Calais. The family's prospects brightened when Henry VIII replaced his tired and paranoid father. At court Thomas jousted and played tennis with the energetic and ebullient young king and became a close leisure time companion. Thomas's value to the king gradually waned, however, and after about 1523 he was less and less prominent in court circles. Now no longer a serious political threat to his monarch, the marquess spent his remaining years enjoying his estates, particularly Bradgate, where he continued the construction of the mansion his father had begun.

In 1519 he wrote to his former tutor, Cardinal Wolsey, from his 'poor lodge at Bradgate'. The term 'poor' is probably less a description of the state of Bradgate and more in deference to the Cardinal, who was much in royal favour and who was engaged on a huge building programme of his own, particularly at Hampton Court. By 1530, the year of Dorset's death, the greater part of Bradgate was probably complete and thereafter only subject to modifications by later generations of Greys.

Accounting for the building and development of Bradgate presents serious problems since our sources of information are very slight. Virtually no documentary records of what was a costly and lengthy operation have survived and evidence from the layout and fabric of much of the ruins is of doubtful value. It thus becomes necessary to compare what we see at Bradgate with the designs, materials and finances available to Dorset's contemporaries of similar rank in other parts of the country.

Thomas, the first marquess, appears to have had at least the basic ideas of what he set out to achieve and these were more or less followed and developed by his son. Civil warfare was at an end and the new house was to was to be one of splendour and (compared to a castle) comfort, with all notions of defence abandoned. In the first place the house was to be sited over two miles away from the ancestral home at Groby, a bold move. Second, there was to be no moat and no great gatehouse. This was an even more daring break with tradition and was in strong contrast to the nearby Kirby Muxloe Castle, started but then abandoned twenty or so years earlier by William lord Hastings, on the site of the family's ancestral manor house. Moreover, Dorset's house would be constructed on only three sides rather than in the form of a hollow square, the familiar layout.

Stone was the traditional material for great buildings, but was rejected at Bradgate in favour of brick. The former was

Brick-making

The Romans made bricks. They were shallow, like tiles, and examples can be seen in the Jewry Wall and (re-used) in the adjoining tower of St Nicholas' Church in Leicester. After the Romans left, the inhabitants of England largely abandoned making bricks and turned to more easily obtainable building materials, such as wood and stone. Brick making continued on the Continent and was introduced into East Anglia in the thirteenth century, probably by Flemish immigrants. The word 'brick' did not enter the English language until the fifteenth century. Until then bricks were usually known as wall tiles. The earliest local example of brickwork is probably at Groby where Thomas Grey, the first marquess of Dorset, began modernising the Old Hall. Other very early examples in Leicestershire are parts of Ashby Castle (c. 1470), Kirby Muxloe Castle (1480-84) and part of the boundary wall of Leicester Abbey (c. 1500). The new building material quickly became fashionable and prestigious, and it is hardly surprising that Thomas Grey chose it for his new house at Bradgate.

One of the problems with using bricks was the difficulty of transporting heavy, bulky material by packhorse on roads too rough for wheeled traffic. Consequently, they could really only be used in quantity where there was a local supply of clay. After being dug up, the clay was left out in the frost over the winter; then it was spread on hay or straw and wetted and trodden to screen out pebbles and other rubble. Next it was placed in wooden moulds and left to dry for a month or so. After that bricks were fired for about a week in an improvised kiln known as a clamp. As temperature control was difficult, the size of the bricks was variable, as is the case of Bradgate House. Patterns such as diapers of diamonds were created by choosing bricks with burnt ends and laying these end-on as headers in the brickwork.

On the south side of Cropston Reservoir, about half a mile from the House, a field known as 'The Dumples' marks the site where the kilns were located. Here three distinct areas of burning have been detected and ploughing still brings to the surface fragments of Tudor bricks. Areas now covered with bushes together with long filled hollows mark the probable site of the clay diggings.

dull grey granite, locally plentiful and well suited to building. But granite walls were the sign of the castle, acceptable for foundations, but otherwise very depressing. Brick on the other hand was fashionable, it could be used to great decorative effect and, not least, was costly to produce and therefore a sign of wealth and status. At considerable cost and effort, stone and also timber were brought from the deserted manor house of the former earl of Warwick at Sutton Coldfield. The end result of all this activity was a house which came to be recognised as perhaps the first truly open country house in England.

The political careers of the Dorsets, father and son, were closely linked to their financial circumstances. Thus, whilst each had a strong motive for building, their means and opportunities for action were subject to considerable change. The records, mostly from official sources, suggest there were three periods of activity at Bradgate. The first was between 1499 and 1507, when the family was relatively free from trouble and when their financial situation was reasonably healthy. During this time Thomas the elder had begun preparation of the site and Thomas the son had probably laid the foundations and started the expansion of the park. After his period in gaol and exile, the latter may have resumed work between 1509 and 1511. Thereafter he was heavily involved in serving the king (Henry VIII) at home and abroad until 1523, when his duties were relaxed and he could spend more time at Bradgate. He died in 1530. His heir, Henry, later to be the father of lady Jane Grey, was a boy of 13 when he succeeded to the lands and title. Any additions, extensions or improvements must have taken place between c.1537, the date of his coming of age, and c.1552 when the Greys moved their centre of political operations to Sheen on the banks of the River Thames and near the royal court.

We must take into consideration a number of other factors when trying to account for the development of the house. Much time and effort had to be spent on the logistics of recruiting and retaining a workforce, skilled or unskilled. Of the former, brickmakers and stone masons in sufficient numbers could not be recruited quickly, and once laid off would disperse to other sites in search of work. The building of kilns and the firing of bricks were skilled jobs with the latter occupying only the winter months. Assembling other materials, such as large timbers, could also be a lengthy task. Actual construction took place between March and October, the cold and frosty months being used by skilled men who could work near the site under some kind of cover. In addition, we do not know how much of the work was supervised by the marquess in person and how much was delegated to his surveyor or steward on site, and indeed how competent these men turned out to be. We can expect the principal craftsmen to have been given considerable discretion in solving technical problems as they arose. We certainly do not know what, if any, marked effect on progress the weather had.

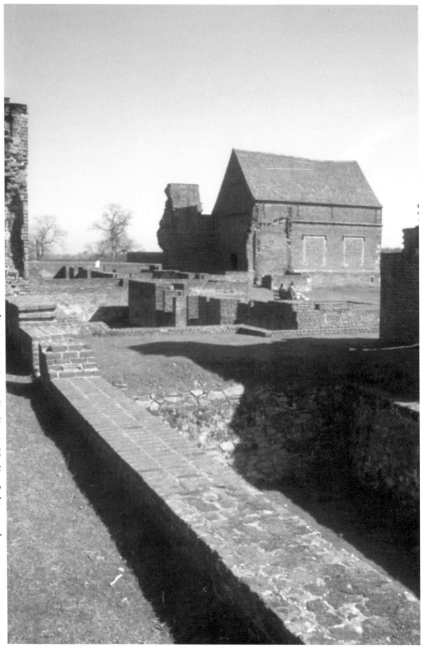

A view across the ruins of Bradgate House. In the forground is the cellar below the sevants hall. Adjoining that was the great hall. The only intact building now standing is the chapel, itself much restored, and given a new roof this century

All available physical evidence suggests that there was no building present at Bradgate before the year 1500 and that the first marquess's contribution was limited to levelling the site. The principal elevation of the house was 200 feet long and faced south. It fronted the great hall, about 80 feet long, which had a fire place and chimney rather than the central fire of a typical medieval hall. A screens passage separated the hall from the service buildings to the west and it seems likely that these form the oldest part of the building and contain reworked timbers from Sutton Coldfield.

The whole household comprised perhaps some 200 people. The senior members of the family dined at a table on a dais at one end of the Great Hall whilst the others ate at tables in the body of the hall. As time went by it became the custom for the family to withdraw to private apartments, which at Bradgate were in the east wing. Most of the houses of this period were built with a range of rooms arranged one room deep. At Bradgate the rooms were double banked which suggests that additions and alterations to the original plan were being made as building progressed.

This sort of development was not unusual in early Tudor houses as seen at The Vine in Hampshire and Compton Wynyates in Warwickshire. What slight evidence there is at Bradgate suggests that the outer bays, each 21 feet wide, were later additions. In this case it is easy to account for 'second thoughts' on the part of the marquess since the building of Bradgate appears to have taken place over the period 1499 to 1507 and possibly 1509 till 1511, with major progress being made between the years 1523 and 1530. The marquess had spent much time in exile in France and was ready to adopt the Renaissance influences which were entering the country through the royal court. Among these was the idea that a house should be symmetrical and the later addition of the corner towers would also greatly add to this effect.

Perhaps such features also reflected the changing fortunes of the Greys and particularly their need to entertain important people and house them and their servants. The provision for guests probably meant that the long gallery was used as temporary sleeping accommodation. This gallery first occupied a position above the east wing but was later relocated to the western side above the bakery.

It is here the problems of interpretation become particularly acute, since attempts at reconstruction, using old and not-so-old materials (mostly from unidentified parts of the main building) have been made. Similar attempts to replace the western walls have gone far beyond anything required simply to make the building safe from collapse. Much cement grouting is visible and almost all the south-westernmost tower has been rebuilt. Moreover, it is doubtful if the ovens in the kitchens are anything more than creative reconstructions. Such attempts at 'imaginative restoration' were taking place as recently as 1929 and, while no doubt done with the best of intentions, now make an accurate interpretation of the fabric difficult.

In 1552 Henry Grey, the third marquess, was created duke of Suffolk, and it is clear that about this time the family came to regard their house at Sheen, on the banks of the Thames and near the royal court, as their main residence.

After the fall of the family in the lady Jane affair of 1554, the estates reverted to the crown. It is likely that Bradgate House was given only the minimum maintenance necessary to keep it weatherproof for a caretaker or tenant. Then, about 1603, Henry Grey, lord Grey of Groby, re-established Bradgate as the family home. After half a century of neglect there was doubtless much need for renovation and improvement. The first earl of Stamford entertained King Charles I for one day in 1634 and similarly in 1697 the second earl received William III, but the records of both visits have also been lost.

Bradgate House

When Bradgate House was built it was at the forefront of English country house design, on a number of counts.

For the first time in many centuries the British nobility felt secure without the need for moats, battlements and thick walls. Bradgate was the first unfortified stately home to be built in Leicestershire.

It was built from brick – a building material which had barely been used in Britain since the Romans left, 1,000 years before.

With its elegant proportions and use of large mullioned windows, Bradgate was an early example of Tudor architecture.

However, in other respects it was firmly traditional. The ground plan of a cross hall flanked by two wings is an ancient design, used for everything from farmhouses to palaces. Also the towers call to mind a medieval castle. Later houses, such as Hardwick Hall, built 100 years after Bradgate, departed from such elements far more thoroughly.

The house was built around three sides of a central courtyard. The Great Hall was originally the dining hall for the whole household – servants and masters. Later the family dined in their living quarters in the east wing.

Over the centuries the house was altered and added to. One notable change was the new bay window added to the Great Hall. this provided panoramic views of the hills to the north, and was built by the 2nd earl of Stamford for the visit of William III in 1696.

A more curious change appears to be the addition of assorted utilitarian buildings across what had been a broad and imposing frontage. The date of these is unknown.

In 1720 the 2nd earl died childless. His cousin, who inherited the title and estates, already had a splendid home of his own in Staffordshire, and saw no reason to remove himself to the old-fashioned house at Bradgate.

When the 3rd earl's son married Mary Booth in 1736, Bradgate was reoccupied by the young couple. Their first two children, including George Harry, the future 5th earl, were born there, and baptised at Newtown Linford church. However, the 3rd earl died in 1739, and his son took possession of Enville Hall and the Staffordshire estates. After three years at Bradgate Henry and his wife clearly felt no desire to linger in, or maintain, their draughty 230 year old mansion. Without an occupant Bradgate fell into disrepair and by the end of the century was no more than a ruin.

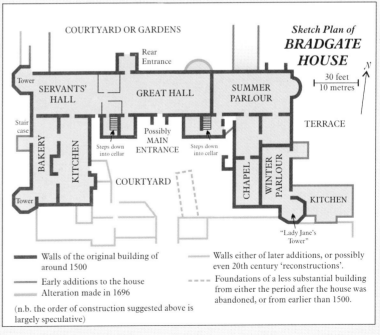

Sketch Plan of
BRADGATE HOUSE

——— Walls of the original building of around 1500

——— Early additions to the house
——— Alteration made in 1696

(n.b. the order of construction suggested above is largely speculative)

——— Walls either of later additions, or possibly even 20th century 'reconstructions'.

- - - Foundations of a less substantial building from either the period after the house was abandoned, or from earlier than 1500.

Where Was the Entrance to Bradgate House?

With very slight documentary evidence, and ruins that have been heavily altered and 'restored', there are many details of Bradgate House that remain very unclear, none more so than the position of the main entrance.

The majority of Tudor buildings have an entrance on the north side, which has led some to suggest the doorway facing Old John was the main entrance.

Alternatively, of the only two contemporary drawings, the map by Kiddiar (see p. 33) shows a major avenue from Cropston, leading some to suggest that guests arrived through an east door, via the garden.

Knyff's engraving, (shown on page 26), on the other hand, shows a broad avenue towards Anstey, to the south, which, combined with the appeal of a dramatic courtyard entrance, and a doorway which would lead directly into the Great Hall, have led others to suggest a main entrance facing the south.

With a period of occupation spanning 230 years it is even possible that the house saw considerable alterations to the layout, including changes to the position of the main entrance.

This reconstruction shows Bradgate House as it may have looked at the time of Lady Jane Grey

Used by kind persmission of Joy Geary and Loughborough University.

Chronology of Bradgate House

1485 – Thomas Grey, 1st marquess of Dorset, returns from France following Henry Tudor's victory at Bosworth Field. In 1488 Thomas sets about improving his manor house at Groby.

1490s – He abandons the work at Groby and makes a start with a new mansion in his expanded deer park at Bradgate.

1501 – Thomas dies with Bradgate only just begun.

1501 – His son Thomas, the 2nd marquess begins serious work on Bradgate House.

1520 – Thomas completes the mansion.

1540s – Lady Jane and her sisters grow up at Bradgate.

1554 – Bradgate is confiscated following the failed attempt by Henry Grey to put Jane on the throne.

1560s – Bradgate is re-granted to the Greys by the crown, but under severe conditions.

1603 – Bradgate and other estates are fully restored to baron Grey of Groby, and at about the same time, Bradgate House is re-occupied.

1628 – Henry Grey is made earl of Stamford.

1634 – Charles I and queen Henrietta visit Bradgate.

1696 – William III visits at Bradgate.

1720 – 2nd earl dies with no surviving childlren His cousin becomes 3rd earl, resident at Enville Hall.

1737 – Future 4th earl is living at Bradgate, where his eldest son was born. He moves to Enville in 1739, on the death of his father.

Mid to late 1700s – Bradgate House falls into increasing disrepair, finally becoming derelict.

1883 – 7th earl dies childless. Bradgate does not follow the earldom.

1928 – Cecily Grey sells Bradgate to Charles Bennion, who presents it to the City and County of Leicester.

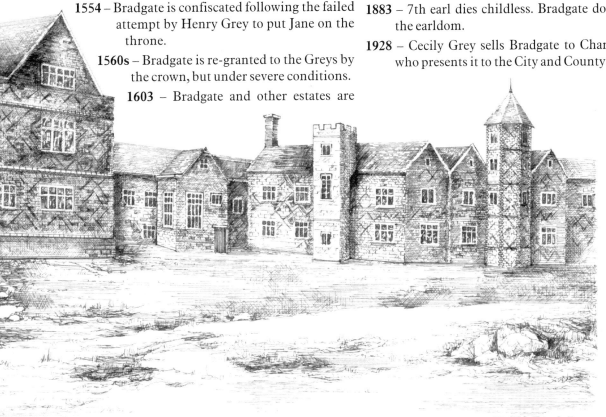

Broadgate in Leicestershire Being the Seate of ye Rt. Honble: the Earle of Stamford.

This drawing by Leonard Knyff is the earliest known illustration of Bradgate House, and dates to about the year 1700, during the time of the second earl of Stamford. The view is from the north, looking towards Anstey. The unfamilar rocky outcrop in the foreground is probably the knoll now covered by the trees of Dale Spinney.

4. THE DEVELOPMENT OF THE PARK.

The first marquess of Dorset had a grand design for his park, which was to furnish a suitable setting to the splendid house while also accommodating the sporting and other recreational needs of the family and guests. Not least, it would proclaim to the whole district and beyond that Thomas Grey was a force to be reckoned with.

The first part of the operation involved the removal of the ancient pale – that is, the bank, ditch and wooden fence which separated the park from the surrounding land and which kept in the deer. This was a long and costly business since the replacement was to stretch over six miles in length, twice as long as the old one. Much of the line of the redundant pale can be detected 'abandoned' within the present park. One such section is crossed by the river and the tarmac drive where Little Matlock gorge opens out at the greensward. (See page 16). At the same time the moated site where the park

---

The Bradgate of John Leland.

'From Leicester to Bradgate by ground well wooded three miles. At Bradgate is a fair park and a lodge lately built there by the lord Thomas Grey, marquess of Dorset, father of Henry that is now marquess. There is a fair and plentiful spring of water brought by Master Brook as a man would judge against the hill through the lodge, and thereby it driveth a mill. The park was part of the old earls of Leicester lands, and since by heirs general it came to the lords Ferrers of Groby, and so to the Greys. The park of Bradgate is a six miles compace.'

Thus wrote the Tudor scholar John Leland (1506-52) on his visit to Bradgate in the 1530s. His description of the Park and Lodge as 'fair' notes his approval and indicates that both were in an advanced state of development if not complete. He also records the presence of the leat taking water from the River Lyn to the house. His description of the length of the perimeter (compace) shows how the park has been reduced in size again, most notably by the reservoir constructed in 1870. Its length now is nearer four miles.

'From Bradgate to Groby a mile and a half much by woodland. There remain few tokens of the old castle other than a hill of the keep that the castle stood on which is very notable; but there is now no stone work upon it. And the late marquess Thomas filled up the ditch, intending to make a herbare (pleasure garden) there. The older part of the work which is at Groby was made by the Ferrers. But newer works and buildings there were erected by the lord Thomas, the first marquess of Dorset; among which works he began he erected the foundation and walls of a great house of brick and a tower but that was left half finished of him, and so it standeth yet. This lord Thomas erected also and almost finished two towers of brick in front of the house, as respondent on each side to the gatehouse.'

The ancient castle of Groby was of the simple motte and bailey type. It had been erected in the late eleventh century, on the site of an earlier structure, and was destroyed about a hundred years later. Thomas Grey had adapted the remains, including the mound which is still extant, to create a garden for the manor house of his Ferrers ancestors. The work at Groby seems to have been abandoned at a late stage in favour of his house at Bradgate.

keeper lived, near the present ruins, was abandoned and the new guardians of the deer were rehoused outside the park.

With the same scant regard to tradition which he had shown with the design of the house and with little thought of expense, the marquess laid out his new boundaries in straight lines across the landscape. The courses of the great north and west pales in particular showed little heed for thoughts of topographical advantage that might reduce the costs of keeping deer in and people out. The road from Newtown to Anstey was re-routed in similar manner and is still followed by the modern road. Later generations of the Greys were to find the upkeep of these ambitious boundaries too costly and, with an eye to the long-term, replaced them with stone walls.

With all these bold actions came problems. The expansion of the park was taking grazing land which otherwise supported the domestic stock of his tenants. A balance had to be struck between their continued ability to pay their rents and their lord's demands for a fine park. Also, the marquess had to ensure that legitimate travellers were able to use the tracks constituting the king's highway across Charnwood Forest, including the ancient route between Newtown Linford and Hunt's Hill (Old John car park).

When Thomas Grey enlarged his deer park, the old boundary pale was left as a bank and ditch within the new park. It can be seen in a number of places. This very marked stretch is in the deer sanctuary area, south of the River Lyn.

Further, there was the matter of access to the common grazing on Charnwood Forest for the stock of the inhabitants of Thurcaston. This was solved by the marquess agreeing to leave a tongue of land leading to the gate, which was the actual point of access and which was located by the modern Hallgates car park.

The first marquess's greatest problem was what to do with the village of Bradgate. He felt that his family and guests should not have to bear the sight of the ordinary people going about their daily grind. Here he was quite ruthless. In league with two more landowners, those two local scions of the Church, the abbot of Garendon and the prior of Ulverscroft, he ordered the demolition of the villagers' houses. It is recorded that they left 'in grief'.

Some of the ridge and furrow of the ploughland of the lost village can readily be seen in the north-east of

the park, to the right of the tarmac drive which leads from Hallgates car park to the deer barns. The locations of the former village houses are much less obvious, (see page 14). Small scattered patches of ridge and furrow can also be found in others parts of the park but, to be fair to the marquess, these were probably abandoned long before he set about his new scheme. By the time the new boundaries of the park had been finalised the ancient hunting park of the Ferrers had been transformed into a park of the times. It covered about a thousand acres and contained the foundations of his proposed mansion.

The first two marquesses were educated men and had travelled in exile abroad. It was probably the higher degree of civilised living they had seen in France which persuaded Thomas the father to introduce unusually advanced facilities to the new house, particularly in the matters of water supply and drainage.

Drinking water was no problem. A spring on the high ground to the north of the house was fed along a pipe by gravity. A larger volume of water, sufficient to flush out the drains under the house and turn the water mill, required a more elaborate solution, for which an unknown but obviously most competent engineer was engaged. In an area outside the pale of the old park, a dam was constructed across the River Lyn. This was close to the well known wishing stone upon which generations of children have been placed and told to make a wish. Behind the dam a sizeable lake was created, stretching towards the present Newtown Linford car park. A ditch-like canal known as a leat was dug and in places banked. It followed the contours of the land from an outlet of the dam and travelled in a wide sweep, allowing just sufficient fall for the water to flow, until it ended in the pond behind the house. This pond provided another head of water to drive the mill, and also serve the fishpond. The leat is still clearly visible along its length, except in the immediate vicinity of the river and across the main drive.

A house fit for a marquess demanded a garden of similar good taste, style and grandeur. Such a garden was indeed laid out but the remains of it today give problems of interpretation similar to those presented by the ruins

This old postcard shows a stretch of the water channel, known as a 'leat', which would have carried water to the house and watermill. Most of the leat remains intact, (see overleaf) but this section was levelled, probably during dredging work on the river.

While the house was occupied there was a dam across the river, probably just beyond the large oak tree in the centre of this picture. This would have raised the water level, allowing it to flow along the leat, which channelled it for about a kilometre (over ½ mile) to a pond behind the house.

LITTLE MATLOCK, BRADGATE.

of the house. The large rectangular area adjacent to the east side of the building, known to later generations as 'the tiltyard', shows many of the typical features of a garden of a 16th century nobleman. Within the high boundary walls raised grassy walkways provided the strolling guests with a view, not only of the delights of the garden but also of the park and its deer beyond. Elegant flights of steps at four points led walkers down to the centre of the garden. Here were the four great parterres – flat, rectangular areas, possibly with flower beds in formal designs or, as Knyff seems to indicate, areas of turf cut into intricate patterns.

Unfortunately such features do not belong only to gardens of the years of the first half of the 16th century. Most could probably be found in many of the fashionable gardens which existed to the outbreak of the civil war a century later. The problems of dating the development of the gardens mirror those with the building of the house. The apparent absence of a prospect mound, a prominent and important feature in

By following the contours along the side of the valley, but descending just enough to keep the water flowing, the leat was able to provide a plentiful supply of water to a point well above the level of the river. The photograph above shows the leat where it approaches Bradgate House. As well as providing for the household needs, and supplying several fish ponds, the water provided power for a watermill. The site, shown on the right, is on the east side of the house, where the water could drive the waterwheel before rejoining the river.

any Elizabethan garden, could be accounted for by the absence of the Greys during the second half of the 16th century. Any developments by Henry Grey (c1510-1554), as third marquess and subsequently duke of Suffolk, have not been detected.

The recovery of the family fortunes in the late 16th and early 17th centuries is reflected in changes in the garden. The Tudor garden was retained by aligning it with the house on an east-west axis. This was achieved by the addition of a second rectangular enclosure of land taken in from the park. It adjoined and lay below that described. At some point it lost its northern boundary wall, but the raised central path is still present. Early air photographs show low planting ridges which may account for the trees on Knyff's drawing made about 1700. Similar beds to the north of the central path can be detected from the air and are also visible on a careful inspection of Knyff's drawing. The realignment was also achieved by the creation of a large rectangular compartment, also taken from the park, which extended along the northern edge of the house and the two gardens. It was subdivided by hedges and fences and had lawns and an orchard. The pond was present, surrounded by bushes and a small spinney. Earlier

fishponds were converted into formal ponds and the leat from the pool was straightened to resemble a canal. To an educated family like the Greys, these features were not only pleasing to the eye but had intellectual meaning.

At some point in the very early 18th century, in the time of the second earl of Stamford and after Knyff's visit, an impressive avenue of trees was planted. It led from the eastern boundary wall of the garden through the park, across land now covered by the reservoir, in the direction of Cropston. This planting was following contemporary developments in the ever-changing fashions of garden design. Unfortunately, it has left no trace on the modern landscape. It is interesting to reflect that it was the effective abandonment of his Bradgate property by the third earl which saved the park from

A view of the garden and the ruins, from the east gate. The rectangular parterres (the sunken area in the centre of the picture), and the raised walkway bordering them, are clearly visible and are typical elements of a Tudor garden.
The house, gardens and formal ponds can be seen, viewed from the north, in the aerial photograph on the previous page.

further major change. Could there be much doubt that had the Greys, ever leaders in fashion, still been resident at Bradgate, they would have called in the services of the leading garden designers of the times, such as 'Capabilty' Brown and Humphry Repton, and thus changed in a major way the landscape of the park? By a stroke of fortune, this historic place has retained much of the world before 1750 for the delight of later generations.

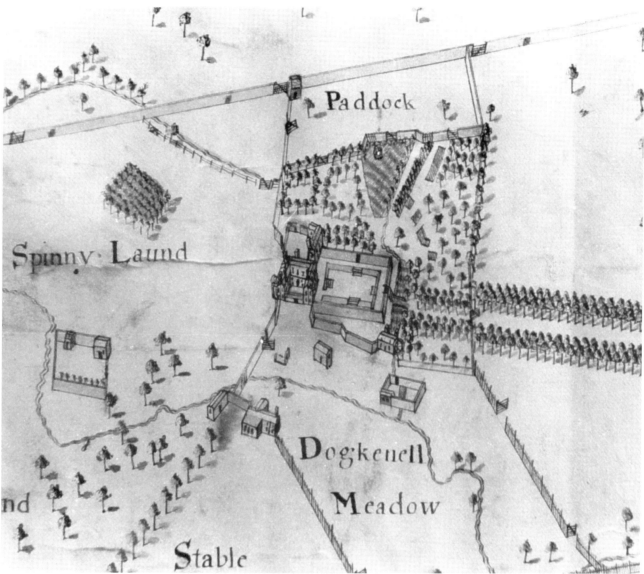

This detail of a map by Nicholas Kiddiar, dated 1746, is, along with Kniff's engraving shown on page 26, the only pictorial evidence we have of Bradgate before the house was ruined. The drawing of the House, confusing though it is, suggests an entrance to the south (towards the bottom of the page). Details of the garden show clearly, as does the splendid avenue of trees leading away to the east – a feature typical of the early 18th century.

Used by kind permission of the Enville Estate.

Overleaf: Part of the canal feature which was added to the gardens in the 17th century.

5. THE GREYS IN TUDOR TIMES

The second marquess of Dorset was a great friend of the young Henry VIII when he was the slim and carefree Prince Hal. A group of high-born young men were always to be found with the prince, playing tennis, shooting at the butts, jousting, hunting and wrestling. Another member of the group was Charles Brandon, with whom Henry's young sister, the Princess Mary, was in love.

After he became king, Henry sent a protesting Mary off to France to marry King Louis XII, an ailing widower of 53. To Mary — young, beautiful and vivacious — it was like being given a prison sentence; but then she looked on the bright side and told her brother that she would marry this time to suit him and next time to suit herself. Sure enough, Louis died after only three months of marriage. Mary was kept in close custody for a time while Louis' successor ensured that she was not in danger of producing an heir. Then Henry sent an envoy to bring her back to England. Oddly, the man he sent was Charles Brandon, duke of Suffolk.

Knowing how his sister felt about Brandon, Henry had taken the precaution of making the duke promise that their relationship would be strictly formal. He reckoned though, without Mary, who greeted the object of her passion with tantrums and floods of tears, begging him to marry her as she was sure she was about to be trapped into some new diplomatic match — which was very likely. Unable to withstand her entreaties, he married her. A great row ensued, but Henry had a way of getting things to work to his advantage. He re-admitted the couple to court on the payment of a heavy fine, which included Mary's dowry, the expenses of her first wedding and all her jewels. This put the Brandons in debt for the rest of their married life. Back in England, Mary and her husband attended the doomed launching of a new warship named after her: the Princess Mary Rose. The wreck of this unfortunate vessel has now been raised from the mud of the Solent.

The Brandons had a son, who died in his early teens, and two daughters, Frances and Eleanor. Frances married Henry, third marquess of Dorset, son of her father's old crony, Thomas Grey.

Henry and Frances were not an endearing couple. Henry had disentangled himself from a contract to marry Katharine FitzAlan, daughter of the earl of Arundel, when the chance of the King's niece came along. He was selfish, weak and ambitious. Frances was arrogant and energetic. Although her place in the line of succession was fairly low, she did not allow people to forget her royal status. She and Henry had three surviving children: Jane, Katherine and Mary.

Henry VIII, by his six wives, also had three children: the Princesses Mary and Elizabeth, and Prince Edward. When Henry died, in 1547, the crown passed to the frail nine-year-old Edward VI.

A king who was a minor always left the way open for manipulative adults to seize control, and this happened again as it had after the death of Edward IV in Elizabeth Woodville's time. It was even worse when there was no clear agreement about the direct line of succession, should the young king not live to provide heirs of his own.

Lady Jane Grey.

Lady Jane Grey was born at Bradgate Park in October 1537, and, according to tradition, was christened in the Parish Church at Newtown Linford. Her arrival was rather eclipsed by the birth the same month of the future Edward VI, followed, two weeks later, by the death of his mother, Jane Seymour.

The Line of Succession

At the time of Edward VI's accession, the next ten people in line for the throne were all female, and there were several interpretations of the order in which they should be ranked. Placing them in what would now be seen as the rightful succession, they were:

1. *Mary Tudor, Henry VIII's eldest daughter (but she had been disinherited under the Act of Succession of 1534, due to the annulment of her father's marriage to her mother, Katherine of Aragon).*

2. *Elizabeth, his younger daughter (but she had been disinherited by her father when her mother, Anne Boleyn, was beheaded).*

3. *Mary, Queen of Scots, grand-daughter of Henry's eldest sister Margaret Stewart, who had married James IV of Scotland.*

4. *Margaret Douglas, daughter of Margaret Stewart by her second marriage. (But both Scottish claimants were discounted to prevent the English crown falling to the Scottish kings; which is, of course, exactly what happened in due course.)*

5. *Frances Grey, elder daughter of Henry's sister Mary.*

6. *Frances' eldest daughter, Jane.*

7. *Frances' second daughter, Katherine.*

8. *Frances' youngest daughter, Mary.*

9. *Frances' younger sister, Eleanor.*

10. *Eleanor's daughter, lady Margaret Clifford.*

Henry VIII's will stated that if the direct line should fail, the crown was to pass to his niece Frances. He was probably not entitled to make such a stipulation, but it brought tragedy both to those who, by their greed, had only themselves to blame, and also to their innocent victims.

From the beginning, Jane's parents had high ambitions for their daughter. They dreamt that one day she would be queen — the wife of her cousin, Prince Edward. Although her parents preferred to spend their days hunting deer, hawking, or stirring up factional conspiracies, they ensured that Jane had every educational advantage. It was the time of the New Learning; the Renaissance of classical culture had spread across Europe during the previous two centuries, and had now reached England. Their daughter had to be made fit for her future role.

Jane, who received little affection from her parents, found her greatest joy in studying. Her father brought a young clergyman, John Aylmer, who later became Bishop of London, to Bradgate to teach his daughter. Jane loved her lessons, and became renowned for her scholarship.

When she was nine, her parents sent her away from Bradgate to learn the ways of the highest society. She therefore joined the Princess Elizabeth in the household of Katherine Parr, widow of Henry VIII, and a woman of fine cultural tastes. After Henry's death, Katherine was still the first lady of the land, and her house became a meeting place for an intellectual sisterhood of high-minded Protestant women. Jane enjoyed the academic environment and also found in Katherine the love and tenderness which were so sadly missing in her parents.

A few months later Katherine Parr married Thomas Seymour, the Lord Admiral (described by Elizabeth as 'a man of much wit and little judgement'). His early morning romps in Elizabeth's bedroom, still in his nightgown and carpet slippers, did not amuse his wife, and Elizabeth was packed off into the country. Jane was a more valuable commodity. The Lord Admiral persuaded her father to pay £2,000 (or at least a few hundred on account) for her to become his ward; in return he would arrange for her to be married to King Edward.

Grey Family Tree: Part one – The Claim to the Throne

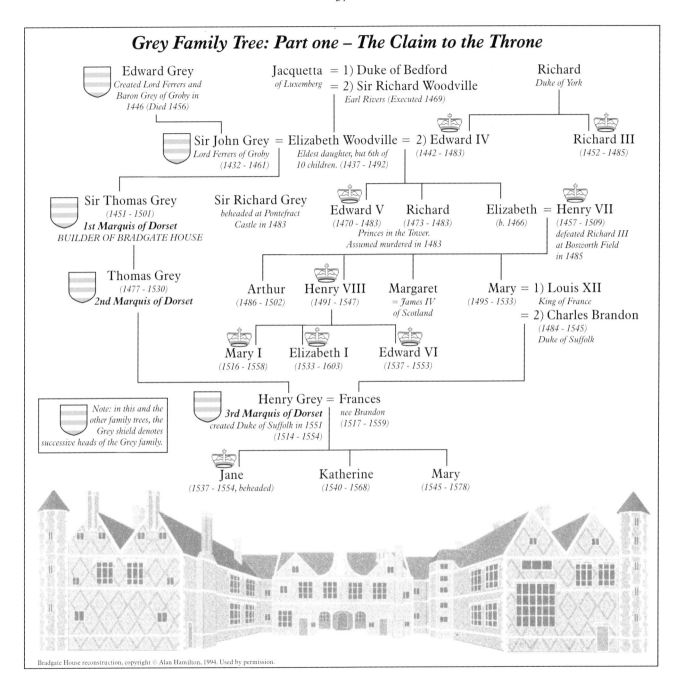

Edward Grey
Created Lord Ferrers and Baron Grey of Groby in 1446 (Died 1456)

Jacquetta = 1) Duke of Bedford
of Luxemberg = 2) Sir Richard Woodville
Earl Rivers (Executed 1469)

Richard
Duke of York

Sir John Grey = **Elizabeth Woodville** = 2) **Edward IV**
Lord Ferrers of Groby / *Eldest daughter, but 6th of* / *(1442 - 1483)*
(1432 - 1461) / *10 children. (1437 - 1492)*

Richard III
(1452 - 1485)

Sir Thomas Grey
(1451 - 1501)
1st Marquis of Dorset
BUILDER OF BRADGATE HOUSE

Sir Richard Grey
beheaded at Pontefract Castle in 1483

Edward V
(1470 - 1483)

Richard
(1473 - 1483)
Princes in the Tower.
Assumed murdered in 1483

Elizabeth
(b. 1466)

= **Henry VII**
(1457 - 1509)
defeated Richard III at Bosworth Field in 1485

Thomas Grey
(1477 - 1530)
2nd Marquis of Dorset

Arthur
(1486 - 1502)

Henry VIII
(1491 - 1547)

Margaret
= *James IV of Scotland*

Mary = 1) **Louis XII**
(1495 - 1533) / *King of France*
= 2) **Charles Brandon**
(1484 - 1545)
Duke of Suffolk

Mary I
(1516 - 1558)

Elizabeth I
(1533 - 1603)

Edward VI
(1537 - 1553)

Note: in this and the other family trees, the Grey shield denotes successive heads of the Grey family.

Henry Grey = **Frances**
3rd Marquis of Dorset / *nee Brandon*
created Duke of Suffolk in 1551 / *(1517 - 1559)*
(1514 - 1554)

Jane
(1537 - 1554, beheaded)

Katherine
(1540 - 1568)

Mary
(1545 - 1578)

Katherine was overjoyed to find she was pregnant and Jane accompanied the couple to their Gloucestershire estate at Sudeley. Here a baby daughter was born, but a week later Katherine died. The young lady Jane Grey, aged 11, was the chief mourner at the funeral of the person she had come to love like a mother.

Jane's parents requested her return to Bradgate and she went home for a while. Then her parents changed their minds and sent the Admiral another £500 for her to go and live with his mother. Gossip had it that Thomas Seymour was planning to marry Elizabeth, or even Jane, himself, but his ambitions and conspiracies had gone too far: he was arrested for treason and executed. Jane went home again.

A famous meeting at Bradgate between Jane and the scholar Roger Ascham was later recorded by him in his book *'The Schoolmaster'*. Ascham, who had known Jane in London, found her alone in the house, while the rest of the household were out hunting. She was reading *Phaedon Platonis* in Greek, and when he asked why she too was not out enjoying herself she replied that all their sport was but a shadow compared with the pleasure she found in Plato.

"One of the greatest benefits that ever God gave me is that he sent me so sharp and severe parents and so gentle a schoolmaster", she explained. "For when I am in presence of either Father or Mother, whether I speak, keep silence, sit, stand or go, eat, drink, be merry or sad, be sewing, playing, dancing, or doing anything else, I must do it as it were in such weight, measure and number, even so perfectly as God made the world; or else I am so sharply taunted, so cruelly threatened, yea presently with pinches, nips and bobs and other ways (which I will not name for the honour I bear them) so without measure misordered, that I think myself in hell, till time come that I must go to Mr Aylmer, who teacheth me so gently, so pleasantly, with such fair allurements to learning, that I think all the time nothing whiles I am with him. And when I am called from him, I fall on

Lady Jane Grey – an engraving from the late 19th century, of a portrait said to be hanging at that time in Bradgate House.

weeping because whatsoever I do else but learning is full of grief, trouble, fear and wholly misliking to me."

Roger Ascham used this encounter in his book to encourage a more humane attitude to teaching children, for it was Alymer's gentleness rather than her parents' harshness which was unusual.

Jane began to write to Aylmer (in Greek), and also (in Latin) to Henry Bullinger, chief pastor of the radical church in Zurich, who encouraged her to learn Hebrew. Bullinger and other Swiss reformers hoped that Jane would marry Edward VI, and steer England into the establishment of a more truly Protestant church.

On one sad day in 1551 Frances Grey's two half-brothers died at Cambridge University of what was probably influenza. Suddenly Frances was heir to the Brandon estates, for her father had died six years before. The marquess of Dorset was given Brandon's title; Henry and Frances were now the duke and duchess of Suffolk. In the same year the powerful John Dudley was created duke of Northumberland. His mother, Elizabeth Grey, was related the Suffolks, and the Greys and the Dudleys were both ambitious. In April 1552 the king became ill with the measles. It soon became clear that tuberculosis had taken hold, and by the next spring he was weak and thin and spitting blood.

John Dudley, duke of Northumberland, realised that the king was likely to die before he could produce an heir. He also knew that under either Mary or Elizabeth he would certainly lose his high position; at worst he would lose his head.

He saw one solution, and that was to wed his last unmarried son, lord Guildford Dudley, to the first eligible female in the line of succession: Lady Jane Grey. The Suffolks were agreeable, and Frances agreed to forego her own superior claim in favour of her daughter. Jane was bullied and abused until she agreed to marry a boy she scarcely knew, and whose father she distrusted.

The wedding took place on May 25 1553 at the Northumberlands' house in London. It was a triple wedding, for at the same time Jane's sister Katherine, aged 13, was married to lord Herbert, and Northumberland's daughter Catherine Dudley married another Leicestershire noble, lord Hastings, son of the earl of Huntingdon, of Ashby de la Zouch Castle. Everything was done in such a rush, that the brides, bridegrooms and their mothers all wore outfits borrowed from the royal store.

Edward knew he was seriously ill, and dreaded a Catholic succession under Mary, so he did not take much persuading to draft a memorandum bequeathing

By tradition the tower on the right of this picture is known as 'Lady Jane's Tower'. As it was the tower adjoining the living quarters it is certainly an area of the mansion that would have been familiar to Jane, as it would to all those who occupied Bradgate House over the centuries.

the crown to Frances Grey, duchess of Suffolk, and her male heirs (for she had not given up hope of producing a son). Then, realising time was too short for that, he changed the wording and bequeathed the realm to the lady Jane. Like his father, he seemed to think he could leave the crown of England to anyone he chose, as if it were just part of his estate. But Henry VIII's 1544 Act of Succession remained on the Statute Book.

Jane now found herself married into a family she hated, and refused to live with them. She was told something of the scheme which was afoot, but refused to believe a word of it, convinced it was all part of a plot to make her return to the Northumberlands. There was a furious row between the two duchesses: Guildford's mother maintained that if Jane would not live with them, her son must go to the Greys. Jane's mother did not want the expense of housing a son-in-law. At length Jane was dragged off to her husband's family once again, where she promptly became ill. She was convinced they were trying to poison her (which shows how little she understood their real motives). She was allowed to go to Chelsea to recuperate.

On July 6th 1553 the king died. Northumberland took control. His plan was to proclaim Jane queen, and then inform Mary that she was disinherited. It was not until three days later, on Sunday July 9th, that the unsuspecting Jane was brought to Syon House, another Dudley residence. On arrival she was amazed and embarrassed when the whole company, including her own parents, knelt before her. Then Northumberland announced that the king was dead and that, as he had disinherited his sisters, Jane was now Queen of England.

This was dreadful news; Jane trembled and sobbed and fell. When at last she could speak, it was to say that the lady Mary was the rightful heir. This did not please the company, who bullied and cajoled her till she gave in, with a typical prayer of submission: "If what hath been given to me is lawfully mine, may Thy Divine Majesty grant me such spirit and grace that I may govern to Thy glory and service, to the advantage of this realm."

The next day Jane was taken down the river to the Tower of London, and entered as a palace the place that became her prison. It was her last journey. In the royal apartments, some of the royal jewels were brought out, including the crown, which was placed on her head. It was explained that another crown would be made for her husband. Jane then realised for the first time the full extent of Northumberland's ambition, and showed that she would never have been the pliant figurehead he had assumed. Her own claim to the throne was tenuous; Guildford's was non-existent. She could make her husband a duke if he wished, she stormed, but never king. A furious family row ensued.

Meanwhile, Northumberland was trying to trick Mary into riding into a trap. He sent a messenger to Hertfordshire, where she was staying, claiming that the king was desperately ill and asking for her. She was saved by Nicholas Throckmorton, who sent her goldsmith to warn her, and instead of riding to London she went to Norfolk, where she had good friends.

On Monday July 10th, 1553 Jane was proclaimed queen in London, and a printed proclamation was prepared for distribution around the country. When a letter arrived from Mary, directing the Council to proclaim her queen, it was clear that they would have to capture her. Northumberland set about raising an army and left London with 3,000 men; Mary had now taken herself to Framlingham Castle in Suffolk where men were gathering to support her.

No battle took place. As Mary's army grew, Northumberland's deserted. The peers realised the way the wind was blowing, and a group of them hastily changed sides, proclaiming Mary in Cheapside. The people went wild with excitement. Church bells pealed, bonfires were lit, and Londoners danced all night. They had no doubt that Mary was their rightful queen, rather than an almost unknown little red-haired girl.

Mary entered London in triumph on August 3rd, with the Princess Elizabeth at her side. Jane and Guildford were kept in the Tower. Northumberland was executed, but Jane's father was granted his freedom after a plea from his wife. There is no record of her mother asking for a pardon for Jane.

Jane and Dudley were allowed a considerable amount of liberty within the Tower. Although she was nominally under sentence of death, Mary knew that Jane was not herself a conspirator, and intended eventually to entrust her to some loyal noble with a suitably remote estate.

Then Mary married the King of Spain. Nothing could have made her more unpopular; it led to war with France and hysteria at home. Plots again abounded.

With a stupidity verging on the insane, Jane's father and his brothers allowed themselves to get involved in a rebellion led by Thomas Wyatt, who marched on London before being defeated. Suffolk and his brother John fled to the old family manor house at Astley, near Nuneaton, and hid in the park, where they were betrayed and discovered: the duke hiding in a hollow tree and his brother under a pile of hay.

This rebellion had nothing to do with Jane. The plan was to supplant Mary with Elizabeth. But Mary's heart hardened and she listened to those who encouraged her to execute her cousin. She gave Jane an escape route; all the stubborn little Protestant had to do was to admit the error of her ways and turn Catholic. When priests were sent to her, Jane engaged them in theological arguments, and prepared herself for death.

When she knew her end was near, Jane sent her Greek testament to her sister Katherine, inscribing it with the advice, "It will teach you to live and learn you to die." She does not appear to have sent a letter to her mother, nor to her husband, who was also to die.

On Monday February 12 1554, Jane watched from her window as Guildford was taken away to public execution on Tower Hill; she was still watching as the cart bearing his body and head, wrapped in a cloth, returned to the Tower.

Jane was granted the privilege of a private execution on Tower Green. She was dressed in black and carried an open prayer book. On the scaffold she made the customary farewell speech; her beloved tutors and correspondents must have been proud when she used the occasion to deliver a short, but impeccably Protestant, sermon.

Her loyal waiting women, Mrs Ellen and Mrs Tilney, assisted her with her clothing and gave her a handkerchief to put over her eyes. She forgave the executioner and asked him to despatch her quickly. When the blindfold was put on, she was unsure where to go, and cried out "What shall I do? Where is it?" She was guided to the block and lay down. The executioner swung his axe and after just sixteen years, lady Jane Grey's life was over.

When the news reached Bradgate that the lady Jane had lost her head, according to legend the woodsmen lopped the tops off the oak trees. Ancient, pollarded oaks are one of the enduring features of Bradgate Park.

Bradgate's Ancient Oaks

It has long been known that the age of a tree can be determined by counting the rings in the trunk. Each summer the tree puts on a little more growth and forms another ring. The disadvantage of this method of dating was always that a tree had to be cut down before the rings were counted. Dendrochronology enables living trees to be dated. It is done by withdrawing a narrow core from the trunk. Not only can the rings be counted in the normal way, but oak timber and living trees can be dated by comparing the rings on the core against a known profile built up from trees whose ages are documented. This is possible because of different growth rates each year, caused by varying weather and other conditions. A warm wet summer will produce a wide ring for instance, while a drought will produce a narrow one.

The oldest tree at Bradgate on which this technique has been used has been dated to 1595, rather later than lady Jane's time. Some of the ancient oaks may be old enough to have been young trees when Jane was executed in 1554.

Dendrochronological data suggests two distinct phases of oak tree planting in the park. The first was in the late sixteenth to early seventeenth centuries, and the second was towards the middle of the eighteenth century, when trees in the previous group would have reached maturity. The Bradgate Park Trust has engaged in further planting in recent years.

One of the reasons why the oaks of Bradgate have lived for so long is the fact that at regular intervals over the centuries the tops have been cut to produce successive crops of poles. Such cropping, above the grazing height for the deer, is called pollarding. It seems most likely that this practice has given rise to the legend that when lady Jane Grey was beheaded the oaks of Bradgate were also 'beheaded'. The year in question, 1554, may very well have been a year when at least some of the oaks in the Park reached the stage where they were due for pollarding.

Far from injuring or weakening the tree, pollarding maintains the tree's vigour since it prevents it from reaching old age which is characterized by decline, decay and finally death. It is noticeable that none of the ancient oaks appear to have been pollarded for very many years.

6. AFTER LADY JANE

On February 17th, 1554, five days after his daughter's execution, Jane's father, Henry the duke of Suffolk, was put on trial at Westminster. Here he was rather unlucky, for his judge was the brother of the girl he had cast aside in favour of Frances Brandon. He was condemned to death, and executed on Tower Hill the following week. Financial troubles, which had dogged him throughout his life, followed him to the scaffold. A man in the crowd asked how he could get the money he was owed. Henry told him to see his officers; at least he didn't have to worry about that any more.

Henry's brother Thomas was also executed, but his youngest brother John, having a Catholic wife to intercede with the queen on his behalf, escaped to continue the Grey succession for four more centuries. Bradgate, for the moment, was confiscated.

Frances Grey caused a sensation by marrying again three weeks after her husband's execution. Her new husband, Adrian Stokes, was not only fifteen years her junior, but he was a member of her own household. They lived close to Bradgate, at Beaumanor, by the village of Woodhouse, but were sometimes able to visit the Court, where Frances's other two daughters were maids of honour to the queen. When she died she was given a full state funeral at Westminster Abbey as befitted her rank.

Although Mary Tudor had disposed of the oldest of the Grey girls, there were still two more to pose a potential threat. To Katherine's distress, her marriage to lord Herbert was quickly annulled by her father-in-law when it became an embarrassing connection.

Katherine's real troubles began when she fell in love with Edward Seymour, son of the late Lord Protector. After the death of Queen Mary, Edward told Katherine's mother he wished to marry her daughter. Frances promised to get Adrian Stokes to write a letter which she would copy and send to Queen Elizabeth, but unfortunately she died before the letter was sent.

Edward's sister Jane then took a hand and encouraged the couple to marry in secret. Early one December morning in 1560, Katherine and Jane Seymour slipped away from court to Edward's house and Jane fetched a minister, who read the marriage service, pocketed his money, and disappeared. The couple were left alone for a short time, but the girls were back at Whitehall in time for mid-day dinner.

After a couple of further short meetings, Katherine began to suspect she was pregnant. She told Edward and his sister Jane, but then everything went wrong. Edward was sent to the continent and Jane died. Katherine was alone and friendless, with a secret which could not be kept secret for long. First she confided in her old friend Bess of Hardwick, who had once been her mother's lady-in-waiting, and had more recently made Katherine godmother to her daughter Elizabeth. Bess had married her second husband in the chapel at Bradgate House, on August 20th 1547 (at two o'clock in the morning, which astrologers had suggested was the most propitious time). Now married to her third husband, the ambitious Bess had no intention of becoming entangled with a foolish girl from a dangerous family.

Next, and worse, Katherine blurted out her troubles to lord Robert Dudley, elder brother of Guildford and later to become earl of Leicester, who was up to his own ears in gossip linking his relationship with the queen with the recent death of his wife.

Robert told Elizabeth, who was furious. Edward was recalled and the pair despatched to the Tower of London. Here Katherine's son was born, and was called Edward after his father. Meanwhile, the Privy Council failed to find proof that a marriage had taken place, but fined the couple and continued to imprison them for their foolishness.

Although they were supposed to be kept separate the keeper of the Tower was sympathetic. When a second son was born, Elizabeth's fury knew no bounds. Edward and his elder son were sent to his mother's house, while Katherine and the baby were moved around. Her last lodging was at Cockfield Hall in Suffolk, the home of Sir Owen Hopton. By this time Katherine was desperately ill with tuberculosis. On January 27 1568 she called Sir Owen and gave him her rings: one with a pointed diamond which Edward had given her when they plighted their troth; her specially made wedding ring with five links of gold; and a ring engraved with a death's head, which she asked to be given, with the others, to her husband, saying, "it is the picture of myself". Then she died, aged 27.

Lady Mary Grey

There was no happy ending for any of the girls who were too close to the throne for their own good. The youngest sister, Mary, was so small that she is sometimes referred to as a dwarf. She, too, contracted a secret marriage, though not an aristocratic one. When she was 19 she married Thomas Keyes, a middle-aged widower who had been chosen for the position of sergeant-porter at court because of his great height. The wedding took place in the porter's rooms at Westminster in August 1565. When Elizabeth discovered, she had Thomas thrown into the Fleet prison, and sent Mary off to the country until, in 1571, her husband died.

Mary was heartbroken, but the following year she was released, and lived in London for her few remaining years till she died in 1578, aged 32. Elizabeth reigned for another thirty years.

Return to Bradgate

After the death of Elizabeth in 1603, James I celebrated his accession to the English throne and ensured his popularity in the right places by granting new honours and restoring old estates. Henry Grey, son of lady Jane's uncle, Sir John Grey of Pirgo, was created baron Grey of Groby, and restored to the old family titles lord Bonville and Harington. He sold Pirgo (now part of the London borough of Havering), and moved to Bradgate Park.

The ornate alabaster monument in the chapel in the ruins commemorates Henry and his wife Anne, daughter of William, lord Windsor of Bradenham. Henry is clad in a complete suit of armour, while his wife wears the ruff and head-dress of the time. The three shields below the figures show the arms of the Grey family on the left and the Windsor family on the right; the centre shield shows both families: Grey impaled on Windsor. Above the tomb is displayed the achievement of arms showing quarterings of eight families in the Grey pedigree: Grey, Hastings, Valence, Ferrers of Groby, Astley, Woodville, Bonville and Harington.

Henry's son John predeceased him, so the next baron Grey of Groby and owner of Bradgate Park was his grandson, another Henry, who gave the family a considerable boost by marrying Anne, co-heir of William Cecil, second earl of Exeter, of Burghley House near Stamford. Anne's father died in 1623, and in 1628 her husband Henry was created earl of Stamford, in acknowledgement of her Cecil inheritance. He was the first of ten Grey earls of Stamford.

Civil War

In 1634 Charles I and Queen Henrietta Maria paid a visit to Bradgate as they travelled from Nottingham to Leicester, and were entertained by lord and lady Stamford. As Civil War loomed, however, the Greys came out solidly for Parliament. Lord Stamford was Lord Lieutenant of Leicestershire, with the county militia under his command. In 1642, with matters

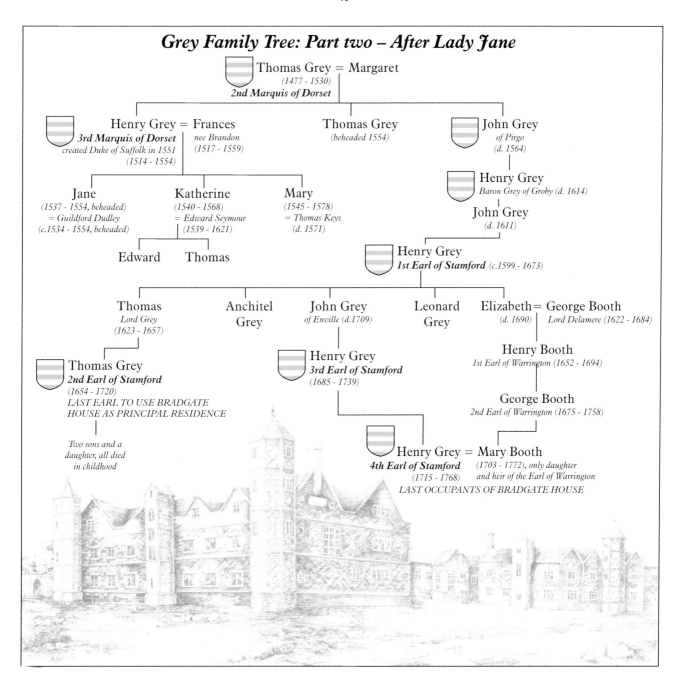

Grey Family Tree: Part two – After Lady Jane

Thomas Grey = Margaret
(1477 - 1530)
2nd Marquis of Dorset

Henry Grey = Frances
3rd Marquis of Dorset
created Duke of Suffolk in 1551
(1514 - 1554)
nee Brandon
(1517 - 1559)

Thomas Grey
(beheaded 1554)

John Grey
of Pirgo
(d. 1564)

Jane
(1537 - 1554, beheaded)
= Guildford Dudley
(c.1534 - 1554, beheaded)

Katherine
(1540 - 1568)
= Edward Seymour
(1539 - 1621)

Mary
(1545 - 1578)
= Thomas Keys
(d. 1571)

Henry Grey
Baron Grey of Groby (d. 1614)

Edward   Thomas

John Grey
(d. 1611)

Henry Grey
1st Earl of Stamford (c.1599 - 1673)

Thomas
Lord Grey
(1623 - 1657)

Anchitel
Grey

John Grey
of Enville (d.1709)

Leonard
Grey

Elizabeth = George Booth
(d. 1690)   *Lord Delamere (1622 - 1684)*

Thomas Grey
2nd Earl of Stamford
(1654 - 1720)
LAST EARL TO USE BRADGATE
HOUSE AS PRINCIPAL RESIDENCE

Henry Grey
3rd Earl of Stamford
(1685 - 1739)

Henry Booth
1st Earl of Warrington (1652 - 1694)

George Booth
2nd Earl of Warrington (1675 - 1758)

Two sons and a
daughter, all died
in childhood

Henry Grey = Mary Booth
4th Earl of Stamford
(1715 - 1768)
(1703 - 1772), only daughter
and heir of the Earl of Warrington
LAST OCCUPANTS OF BRADGATE HOUSE

clearly coming to a head, he was anxious to get control of the arms which were kept in the Magazine, otherwise known as the Newarke Gateway. While he was there the king arrived unexpectedly in town, causing the earl to make a hurried departure, leaving his son and a group of twenty-five officers and men barricaded inside. This defiance annoyed the king, but with only a small troop in attendance there was little he could do.

The leading citizens of Leicester were in a dilemma, not wishing to upset either side and hoping everything would blow over. Eventually, as a compromise, it was agreed to distribute the weapons and ammunition around the county.

On August 22 1642 Charles raised his standard at Nottingham, and the war began in earnest. The Hastings of Ashby de la Zouch, who were more or less permanent enemies of the Greys and on opposing sides during every civil dispute from the Wars of the Roses to the Jacobite Rebellion, seized their chance. Four days after the war began, Colonel Hastings stormed Bradgate with a troop of Royalists. No great damage was done, but some arms and ammunition were taken, as were, for some reason, the chaplain's clothes. At any rate, everybody in residence was very frightened.

Lord Stamford was sent to the west country in command of Parliamentary troops, while his eldest son, Thomas, lord Grey of Groby, took charge of the north midlands, including Leicestershire.

As time went on the earl became increasingly disenchanted with the war. He was plagued with gout, his generalship was criticised, and he was blamed for the loss of the west country. What is more, he complained, his house had been ransacked and his tenants plundered so that they could not pay their rent; he had recruited a regiment at his own expense and was now short of money. He begged Parliament for a grant of £1,000 and leave to travel to France for the good of his health. This was granted.

The real fanatic of the family was lord Stamford's eldest son, Thomas. He revelled in the excitement, and counted himself particularly fortunate to be in direct opposition to Colonel Hastings. As commander of all the Parliamentary forces in Leicestershire, he saw to the garrisoning of Leicester, took a company to save Gloucester, and won a battle at Newbury on his way to London. While his father was pleading for money, lord Grey was content with a letter of thanks.

Leicester was besieged by the Royalists, and almost laid to waste. Ashby Castle, on the other hand, was besieged by Parliament. When the war at last came to an end, Thomas, lord Grey of Groby, sat on the commission which tried and condemned Charles I. 'Tho Grey' was the second signature on Charles's death warrant, between the names of John Bradshawe and Oliver Cromwell. He was nominated to the new Council of State, but already had a reputation as a trouble maker and was kept out of Parliament. Cromwell distrusted him. After involving himself in various lunatic groups such as the Fifth Monarchy Men, and spending time in the Tower, lord Grey died in 1657.

Lord Stamford outlived his son by many years and, losing patience with the Commonwealth, came down in favour of the Restoration of the Monarchy. This meant that he, too, spent time in the Tower. The accession of Charles II brought some relief, but the Greys were always distrusted by the Stuarts. When the earl died in 1673, he was succeeded by his grandson, another Thomas.

Fire at Bradgate

The second earl of Stamford inherited his share of the recklessness which afflicted the family at this period. Bradgate was suspected of being a centre of treacherous activity and searched for arms. Thomas became involved in the duke of Monmouth's Rebellion: a plan to supplant the unpopular catholic King James II with one of Charles II's illegitimate sons. He was arrested at

Bradgate and sent to the Tower for a while before being included in a general pardon.

The Glorious Bloodless Revolution of 1688, which brought William and Mary to the throne, improved lord Stamford's fortunes. He married Elizabeth Hervey, whose father had just died and left her £100,000. The attractions of Bradgate were lost on Elizabeth, who did not enjoy being stuck in the middle of a deer park, and wrote to her sister that although the house was tolerable, the country was a forest. and the inhabitants all brutes. Her sister, according to tradition, wrote back suggesting she set fire to the place and run away by the light thereof.

There was certainly a fire, which apparently began in the north west tower where the earl slept, but as the countess and her baby daughter only narrowly escaped with their lives, it seems unlikely that she deliberately started it. However, lord and lady Stamford were divorced. The earl found another heiress, Mary Maynard, and married again.

This picture, taken from inside the ruins, shows the position of the Great Hall, with cellar below. The largest window was a bay, which was specially built for the visit of William III in 1696.

King William's Visit

The great event at Bradgate at this time was the visit of William III in the summer of 1696. The Stamfords were desperately keen to impress the king, hoping he would shower honours and riches upon them. No expense was spared: stables for a hundred horses were erected in the Park; one of the bridges over the brook at Anstey, known ever since as King William's Bridge, was widened to accommodate the king's carriage; and a great new bay window was inserted into the great hall at Bradgate House. This was for a visit which lasted one day. The king was pleased by all he saw and thanked the Stamfords for their hospitality, but they never recovered financially from their extravagance.

The second earl was described in 1705 by a contemporary who said, "He doth not want sense; but by reason of a defect in his speech wants elocution; is a very honest man himself, but is very suspicious of everybody who is not of his party, for which he is very zealous; jealous of the power of the clergy, who, he is afraid, may some time or another inflame our Civil Government. From a good estate he is become very poor, and much in debt. He is something above middle stature; turned of fifty years old."

Thomas Grey, second earl of Stamford, died without direct heirs in 1720. There is a slate memorial stone to him and his second wife Mary in the floor of the Chapel in the ruins.

Rabbits

Rabbits were introduced into Britain by the Normans and, until the outbreak of myxomatosis in the 1950s, were always very plentiful in Bradgate. In the middle ages and beyond, rabbits – more usually known as conies – were kept in enclosures called warrens. They were carefully fed and protected as a source of food for the warrener's owner at all seasons. Fences, banks and walls prevented the animals from escaping. Those individuals which did gain their freedom seldom lived long in the wild, where hordes of predators, human and animal, eagerly took them.

The site of the main warren at Bradgate, marked on early maps as 'the Cunnery' and now under the reservoir, produced phenomenal numbers of animals in its time. In the five months from September 1759 to February 1760, for example, 2,255 couples were removed. In the early 1800s it was run by a warrener, one Henry Webb, who was paid nine shillings (45p) a week for his services. He was expected to maintain a stock of rabbits at all times and to meet whatever demands were made by his employers in terms of meat and skins. In good years and with skilful management this was no problem. His rabbits bred mostly between January and June. Does mated as young as six months and had their young four weeks later. Moreover, most mated and conceived again only twelve hours after giving birth. Litters were around seven and seldom less than three and some females produced as many as sixty offspring each per year. Apart from predators and disease, Webb's main problem was bad winters when large numbers had to be fed, largely on turnips, to prevent starvation. In later years the warrener employed assistants to catch the rabbits which had escaped from the enclosure and had established themselves in other parts of the park. Regular catching places called 'pitches' produced huge numbers of additional animals. Although the numbers caught did vary, the price the animals fetched remained remarkably constant. In Webb's time a couple in good sound condition were worth 18d (7½p). Poorer stock fetched 9d (4p) a couple. The profit in 1822 from rabbits from the park was £82.

There were several commercial warrens on Charnwood Forest outside Bradgate and not all were expertly managed. Rabbits regularly escaped from their enclosures in such numbers that they were even able to establish wild colonies on the open moorland. Here they competed with domestic stock. The close cropping and incessant nibbling of the rabbits reduced the value of the sheep walks to almost nil. When the rabbits turned their attention to the crops of the local people there was such an outcry that the warrens were eventually closed. At the same time changes in agricultural practices and the persecution by gamekeepers of the rabbits' natural predators allowed the populations to extend their range. Thus the rabbit secured a place as a familiar animal in the countryside. In the late nineteenth century rabbit shooting in the park by lord Stamford and his friends was part of the sport. In the 1850s daily totals for January shoots were from 1474 to 3075. In December 1861 a party of thirteen guns killed 3,333 rabbits in one day. In 1953 myxomatosis swept through the park and reduced the population to a few hundred individuals. More than forty years on the populations are once more rising but are still far from their pre-disaster levels.

7. THE DECAY OF BRADGATE HOUSE

*A*s none of the second earl's children survived, on his death his estates passed to his cousin Henry, who lived at Enville Hall, near Stourbridge, in South Staffordshire. The new lord Stamford seems to have been a particularly unpleasant character. He drank heavily and beat his wife, who eventually left him. Being settled in a house which had belonged to other branches of the Grey family for many generations, he seems to have had no interest in either living at Bradgate or in selling it.

Despite their tempestuous marriage, the third earl and countess produced two sons and five daughters, as well as three children who died in infancy. A significant event in the family fortunes took place in 1736 when lord Stamford's heir, Harry, lord Grey of Groby, married a kinswoman, lady Mary Booth, daughter of the 2nd earl of Warrington.

The chances of this being a happy union would not have seemed high. For a start, the bride, at 33, was 12 years older than her husband, and both parties had seen their mothers (married for their money) either battered or scornfully rejected. Mary Booth, an only child and therefore an heiress, was the apple of her father's eye. Lord Warrington kept her as his companion at the family seat, Dunham Massey, near Altrincham, Cheshire, until his desire to ensure a succession overcame his reluctance to part with her. His grandmother, lady Elizabeth Grey, was a daughter of the 1st earl of Stamford, and the Greys and Booths were both for Parliament in the Civil War, so it appears the liaison was arranged by the families. It seems to have been a great success.

The Greys and Booths between them now owned three major estates, at Dunham Massey, Enville, and Bradgate. So it was to Bradgate that the young couple came to begin their married life, putting some space between them and their various parents for at least part of the year. The house was opened up and refurbished, and the year after their marriage their union was blessed by the birth of a son and heir. George Harry Grey was baptised at Newtown Linford Church on October 21st 1737. Eighteen months later a daughter, Mary, was also born at Bradgate, and baptised at Newtown Linford Church on April 30th 1739.

This last occupation of Bradgate House was happy but brief. In November 1739 the 3rd earl of Stamford died at Enville, and Harry and Mary came into their Grey inheritance. They moved to Enville Hall, and Bradgate House was finally abandoned.

When the house was boarded up, the furniture must have been moved out, possibly to Enville. If no proper maintenance was taking place, every winter would make its depredation. Slates would be blown off the roof, letting in the rain; brick walls, in need of repointing, would become unsafe; perhaps the final straw was something like the breaching of the dam and the collapse of the water and drainage system. In 1800 an old man related how in his youth the house had been complete, but by then it was a ruin, though the walls and towers were higher than they are now. Once slates and bricks were to be had for the carrying, local people were not slow in finding other uses for them. Look at the nearby villages of Newtown Linford, Cropston and Thurcaston, for example, and notice how many timber-framed houses are infilled with beautiful hand-made bricks, just like those at Bradgate House!

Newtown Linford churchyard contains the graves of several stewards, whose task it was to look after the Park: John Marston, who died in 1724; Daniel Lambert, who died in 1761; and another Daniel Lambert, perhaps his son, who was the uncle of Leicester's famous fat man.

Enville Hall

Enville Hall near Kinver, South Staffordshire, belonged to a branch of the Grey family from about 1500. When the second earl of Stamford died childless in 1720 his cousin Henry, who inherited the title, was already Master of Enville, and never lived at Bradgate House, which was abandoned. Enville became one of the two principal seats of the family (with Dunham) until the twentieth century.

It was rebuilt after a fire in 1904 and is still a private house, having passed to the relatives of Catherine Cocks, seventh countess of Stamford and Warrington, on her death in 1905.

Dunham Massey

The Dunham estates, near Altrincham in north Cheshire, came to the Greys as a result of the marriage in 1736 between Harry, fourth earl of Stamford, and Mary Booth, daughter and heiress of George Booth, earl of Warrington. Successive earls have made their mark on Dunham Massey down the centuries. It stands in a deer park which is reminiscent of Bradgate. In the nineteenth century staff sometimes interchanged between the family estates, and management practices could be shared, particularly while William Martin was agent of all the Grey lands.

The tenth and last earl of Stamford lived at Dunham until shortly before he died in 1976, after which, as he had arranged, the estate passed to the National Trust. The house contains numerous family portraits and other memorabilia and, along with its park and gardens, is open to the public. There is a restaurant and shop in the stable block.

For the next 150 years a succession of four eldest sons were named George-Harry in order to reflect both family traditions: George for the Booths, Harry for the Greys. The importance of the Booth inheritance was recognized when the title earl of Warrington was revived for Mary Booth's son, who became earl of Stamford and Warrington.

This George Harry, who had been baptised at Newtown Linford, made a good marriage, linking the Greys to one of the country's most prominent families. His bride was Henrietta Cavendish Bentinck, whose brother, the third duke of Portland, became Prime Minister. The Grey family fortunes fluctuated down the years as new sources of wealth were carefully garnered by some generations, only to be squandered by dissolute heirs. Both the sixth earl and his son, who predeceased him, suffered ill health with bad grace, with disastrous effects on their marriages.

Old John

In 1786 the coming-of-age of the future sixth earl was celebrated at Bradgate by a bonfire on the highest point of the park, on a hill which was already shown as 'Old John' on a map of 1754. There had been a windmill on this site in the 1740s. It may have been a post mill, the oldest windmill design, in which the whole of the mill and its machinery rest on a single post, so that it can turn, along with the sails, to face the wind. No trace of it remains.

Old John Tower, by popular legend a beer mug memorial, was in reality a folly, beginning life as a 'ruin', later being converted into a viewing tower for horse racing.

From the Diary of Viscount Torrington

John Bing, viscount Torrington, visited Bradgate on his travels through England in the late eighteenth century.

"Tuesday 8th June 1790. We left Leicester at eleven o'clock ... along a true Leicestershire road, of stones and sloughs ... (which) ... brought us to the village of Anstey and soon after to the confines of Bradgate Park. Bradgate has been dismantled of its timber and its keeping (flock of sheep) tho' yet stocked with deer; and the house was long since burnt. It was, I conclude, and might be restored to, I am certain, a noble place; for the grounds are very bold and diversified, and a trout stream capable of any formation twines thro' the valley; but it would require a great sum to render it complete. Beneath the ruins and within old walls, Ld Stamford's foxhounds, a noble and celebrated pack, are kept; these I saw, and honour'd with my approbation. Ld Stamford has a hunting seat at two miles distance." (Stewards Hay)

Torrington also went on to Ulverscroft where he lamented the actions of the local farmers who 'destroy wantonly' the ancient building.

(Source; 'Rides Round Britain John Byng, Viscount Torrington. Ed. Donald Adamson Folio Society 1996)

This engraving of the ruins, dated 1793, much the same time as when Viscount Torrington was passing by, shows the ruinous state of Bradgate House, 53 years after the Grey family finally moved out. The depleted state of the brickwork implies wholesale quarrying of the bricks, many of which can be seen in the houses of surrounding villags.

(Engraving from J Nichols, vol IV, 1807-1811)

The Walls of Bradgate

None of the walls in the park dates from its creation by Thomas Grey. The external boundaries of his 'new' park of c. 1500 were originally laid out with a ditch and bank topped with the traditional wooden paling. However, these were taken down in the 1740s to be replaced and augmented by the walls we see today. Oak paling had proved too expensive or difficult to replace after the Greys had abandoned the house and moved to Enville in Staffordshire.

The great walls marking the northern and western boundaries were largely the work of two men, William Coulson and Thomas Sketchley. In 1741 Coulson received 2½d (1p) a yard for building 5623 yards (3.19 miles, 5.1 km) of wall. The previous year, 5771 yards had been constructed, probably by the same man or by the same team. Much of the total for the two years must have included the great central wall which now divides the 'High' Park from the 'Low' Park. A great deal of the south-east and south-west walls was erected between 1790 and 1795 and was probably the work of Thomas Sketchley.

Between about 1831 and 1841 the sixth earl of Stamford established the now familiar spinneys in the High Park. They were planted primarily for the furtherance of pheasant shooting rather than for the benefit of the deer. The walling round these areas was started about 1828 and was the work of the celebrated Charles Firth, who appears to have spent most

of his long working life on the Bradgate estate.

The repair and general maintenance of so many miles of wall was a perennial activity. In 1740 William Lovet was paid 4 shillings (20p) for turfing four acres (ie. furlongs) of walling. Sixty-eight years later, a member of the local family of Rudkin earned £2.10.2d (£2. 51p) for capping and turfing 220 yards (200 metres) of the park wall. In the 1860s members of the same family, together with a team of men, were receiving 8s.10d (44p) a yard for similar skilled work.

The work of dating the walls has also come from a study of lichen flora growing on the individual stones. Colonies of different species become established and expand in a well recognised sequence of 'pioneer' open and 'stable' closed communities. The same technique can sometimes be used to date the walls of old buildings.

The well-known legend of Old John states that at the celebratory bonfire, a central pole in the fire burnt through and fell, killing the popular but possibly inebriated miller, who has become associated with the name Old John. To commemorate the old man and his weakness for alcoholic liquor, so the story goes, a hunting tower was built and was shaped like a beer mug. The truth is more confusing. Contemporary estate accounts record that Old John Tower was built in the autumn of 1784, two years before the celebration bonfire. The original tower, built by Thomas Sketchley of Anstey, appears to have been an open 'folly', or mock ruin, similar to that at Mow Cop in Staffordshire. Early photographs show a second apperture and beyond that

more stone walling. These were removed during alterations undertaken in the mid 19th century by the seventh earl of Stamford and Warrington, when he laid out a practice circuit for his race horses around Old John. The tower was made into a viewing place, complete with fireplace, carpet and many home comforts. A stable block, where horses could be rubbed down, was built into the hillside, where a brick wall can still be seen. During the nineteenth century the 'ruined

wall' beyond the main archway became progressively smaller, resulting in the familiar 'beer mug' we see today.

William Martin, ancestor of Sir Robert and Sir Andrew Martin, who were to give such outstanding service as Chairmen of the Trustees of Bradgate Park, became agent for the Bradgate estates in 1793, when he was only eighteen. He served the Grey family for the next fifty-five years, eventually taking charge of all their estates.

The fourth, fifth and sixth earls of Stamford (George-Harrys all) divided their time between Enville, Dunham and their London house; the Leicestershire estates were primarily a source of income.

In 1842, Queen Adelaide, widow of William IV, celebrated her fiftieth birthday by having a picnic in Bradgate Park. She herself chose the site for the picnic — under an ancient tree between the ruins and the stream. It afterwards became known as Queen Adelaide's Oak, shown below.

The Deer

It is very likely that there have been deer in Bradgate without a break since before the year the park was first noted, in 1241. Indeed, it was to preserve the deer for hunting that the original park was created by the Ferrers, Lords of Groby. To contain the deer, this earlier park was surrounded by a bank and ditch, some of which can still be seen within the present park. A well preserved section of the same bank remains beneath the water of the reservoir. (See aerial photograph on page 14.)

There are two species of deer at Bradgate: the red and the fallow. The red deer is the largest of Britain's wild mammals and, although really an animal of woodland, it is most usually thought of as roaming the hills and mountains of the north and west. The males are called stags and the females hinds. During the summer months, the males have deep-brown or reddish-brown coats, darker on the underside, with a light yellowish area around the base of the short tail. In winter the coats become darker and thicker. Adult stags have antlers which are used for fighting. Each spring they shed them and over the following four months grow new ones. The furry skin covering them is called 'velvet' and is rubbed off against a tree or rock.

The hinds do not have antlers, and have their young, the calves, in early summer. Each is left in a safe place during the day while the mother feeds. As time goes by the young one learns to follow its mother around until it can fend for itself.

For most of the year the older stags live in separate herds from the hinds and the young stags. In October and early November the sound of the red stags roaring can be heard in the Park. This is the 'rut' or breeding season, when each stag gathers together a group of hinds and defends them with great determination. Challenges are met with the clash of antlers and rival stags become locked in contests of strength and stamina. Visitors should be very wary of approaching deer at this time.

Fallow deer are smaller than red deer. The males are called bucks and reach a height of about one metre at the shoulder. Their antlers are more flattened and less pointed than those of the red deer, and the easiest way to tell the two species of deer apart is by looking at their antlers (see the diagrams opposite). Fallow deer shed their antlers in late spring, and they are about eight years old before the antlers reach their full size. In the summer the fallow deer have coats which are reddish-brown dappled with large white spots, and the tail area, known as the rump, is white, outlined in black. In winter the coat becomes grey-brown with light underparts.

The female fallow deer is known as a doe and her young are called fawns. As with red deer, they are usually found near the bucks at rutting time in late autumn, but unlike the red deer, fallow deer live in mixed herds of bucks and does all winter.

For the last two hundred years at least there have numbered upward of 300 deer on the Park, roughly half red and half fallow. The chief limiting factor has always been the amount of grazing available. In the nineteenth century, the deer competed with domestic grazers for the limited supply of food. These included horses, Galloway cattle, bulls, sheep, goats, mules and even llamas. Measures are being taken to control the bracken which spreads over open areas, crowding out the grass. Formerly local farmers, tenants of the Bradgate estate, were allocated a strip of bracken, which they cut and stored in 'fern stacks' to use for winter bedding.

In the past, hard winters have seen deer perish in large numbers. In 1812 turnips were given, and today regular winter feeds of hay are provided.

Annual cycle of red deer

The inner ring shows Hind (female) activity. The outer ring shows the Stag behaviour

Red Deer

- Cast Antlers
- Grow new antlers
- Calves born
- Clean velvet from antlers
- Rutting Season
- Rutting Season
- Stag herds form
- Hind herds form

Red deer antler, 6th head

Annual cycle of fallow deer

The inner ring shows Doe (female) activity. The outer ring shows the Buck behaviour

Fallow Deer

- Herds
- Cast antlers
- Fawns born
- Grow new antlers
- Clean velvet from antlers
- Rutting season
- Rutting season

Fallow deer antler, 6th head

Bradgate Revisited

In 1845 the Grey family title passed to the eighteen-year-old George-Harry, grandson of the sixth earl, and Bradgate made a come-back.

The seventh earl was an immensely wealthy young man when he succeeded, with a rent roll of £90,000 a year. All the society mothers with daughters to place had their eyes on him. Instead, he eloped to Brighton with Bessie Billage, the daughter of the bootman at his Cambridge college. Poor Bessie never took to being a countess. When her husband took her to Enville, she could not get out of the habit of curtseying to vicars' wives, and calling them madam. As she was clearly unhappy, George-Harry took a house at Hove where they lived for a while; then he got restless and began to go off on sporting trips with his friends. He was fishing in Scotland in 1854 when he received a telegram to say that Bessie had died of a seizure.

The hopeful society mamas knew they must let a year's mourning period pass before they could again parade their daughters. Before that time was up, however, George-Harry had found himself another scandalously unsuitable bride. This was Catherine (or Kitty) Cocks, who came from Sturminster Marshall in Dorset. Kitty was the fifth of seven children of a farmworker father and a gipsy mother. One of her brothers was already in gaol for horse stealing, and her

This photograph, probably dating from late in the 19th century, shows the ruins with the gable end of the west wing still intact. This blew down during a gale in 1896. Many of the walls in the picture are of dry stone. It seems likely that bricks from the gable end were used to reconstruct some of these walls.

The Spinneys of Bradgate

As early as the mid eighteenth century successive earls of Stamford had well organised routines for hunting, shooting and fishing over their estates in four counties. When resident in Leicestershire the family lived at Stewards Hay which was close to the site of the present quarry company's offices by the A50 near Field Head. The Greys were wealthy and well placed in Victorian society. As such, they entertained a great deal, sharing with their more sporting guests their passion for shooting.

The pastime of shooting for pleasure developed in the early 1700s and reached a peak of popularity in the late nineteenth and early twentieth centuries. Many of the inclosed Charnwood woodlands, and most of the open hilltops such as those at Bradgate seem to have been used for shooting.

After the enclosure of Charnwood by Act of Parliament in 1808 much of the land concerned came into the hands of the Greys. The fifth and sixth earls of Stamford lost no time in planting up some of the bare slopes in order, as much as anything, to improve the prospects for game. At the same time the high park area of Bradgate was planted with the series of spinneys we see today. A team of keepers was responsible for providing birds for the guns for the season which opened at Bradgate in October and ended in February, or earlier if the supply of game ran

out. The usual species shot were pheasant, partridge and rabbit. The numbers of these accounted for by up to ten guns shooting over four to ten days could run to several thousand. Twelve seasons in the late nineteenth century saw over 40,000 pheasants and 7,000 partridges fall to the guns. During the same period upwards of 75,000 rabbits were despatched. One day one fortunate marksman killed seven with one shot. The plantations in the high park were carefully sited so as to enhance and extend a day's shooting. At the start a chosen spinney was beaten so that the birds were encouraged to escape by taking wing in the direction of a second selected one. In the space between the two the guns were in line waiting to take their toll. The same procedure was adopted between spinneys two and three and so on until a satisfactory day's sport had been declared. Other species such as hares, woodcock and snipe, which were also incidentally involved, also fell to the hunters. As late as 1850 there were still a few black grouse in the park but, perhaps not surprisingly, they disappeared shortly afterwards.

sister Tamar had produced three illegitimate children in the workhouse when real disaster struck. The family's thatched cottage burnt down and their father died of his burns. Their mother was taken into the workhouse until she was expelled for bad behaviour and sent to Bridewell.

Catherine, at twenty, was left with two young sisters to look after. Endowed with only their dark-eyed gipsy beauty and their skill with horses, the three of them went to London to seek their fortunes. Here they fell in with Jem Mason, who owned stables in Oxford Street. The girls broke in ladies' horses and became an equestrian circus act, leaping through hoops of fire.

Catherine became attached to Percy Fielding, a younger son of the earl of Denbigh. Fielding went off to fight in the Crimea, leaving Catherine pregnant. She gave birth to a daughter, also named Catherine, in October 1854, and by the following spring was back at Jem Mason's stables. Here she caught the eye of the newly widowed George-Harry. He fell in love with her, and Kitty Cocks, daughter of a gipsy, sister of a horse thief, mother of a secret daughter, became countess of Stamford and Warrington.

Catherine was a very different character from Bessie Billage. If the staff and tenants at Enville expected another diffident and tearful girl, they found instead a composed and elegant woman. Catherine could play to perfection any part which fate presented to her. She became the gracious lady bountiful, the supporter of worthy charities, the loving wife and the affectionate aunt of her sisters' illegitimate offspring, whom she brought to live under the extensive roof of Enville Hall. Her own little Catherine was secretly fostered with a nearby farming family, and later, it is said, married to a Leicestershire farmer. Her existence was never divulged to lord Stamford, who himself had at least one illegitimate offspring unknown to his wife, but their marriage did not produce children.

The 7th earl was a great sportsman, excelling at cricket and anything to do with horses. In 1855 a request came from the Quorn hunt that he should be its new Master. Having accepted the honour, he set up a pack of hounds and built up a stud of over eighty horses, with the necessary kennels and stables. If he was to spend a good deal of time in Leicestershire he also needed somewhere suitable to live during the hunting season. His agent William Martin had just died, so he decided to use the site of his house, Steward's Hay, near Field Head, for a new mansion. This vast brick Victorian pile, was called (confusingly) Bradgate House. The stables alone cost £30,000, and the house employed twenty indoor servants — two just to dress lady Stamford.

The new Bradgate House at Stewards Hay, near Field Head, straddled the parish boundary bewteen Newtown Linford and Groby. It was built in the 1850s, and had as many windows as there are days in the year. In 1925 it was sold to a quarry company and was demolished. The stable block survives in a derelict state.

The Water Meadow

A water meadow was a system to gain the benefits which natural flooding can give to a grassland meadow, in a controlled way. By using water from a nearby stream to flood over the flat meadow in the early spring, nutrients will be deposited, and ground frosts will be avoided. In these ways an early growth for grazing animals can be provided.

At Bradgate the water meadow is the flat, usually green area between the ruins of Bradgate House and the deer barn, on the south side of the main drive. By using a system of sluice gates water could be channelled from the River Lyn, along the substantial walled ditch that still runs a few feet from the tarmac drive.

At key intersections, such as the one shown in the photograph below, the sluices (now gone) directed the water along a system of brick-lined channels. When these were full the water flowed slowly over the grass on the very gentle slope, eventually rejoining the River Lyn. This form of irrigation was known as 'floating downwards', since the land involved had to be below the level of the take-off point of the water.

The system was introduced to Bradgate in the nineteenth century, and large amounts of money were spent on its construction and maintenance. Although it has not been in operation for many years it is still that part of the park where deer can be most readily seen grazing.

George-Harry's time with the Quorn was not an unqualified success. For one thing, he was expected to take on the full expense of the hunt. Bradgate House was also too distant from the hub of social life at Melton Mowbray. But much of the trouble was due to the attitude of local gentry, particularly the women, to lady Stamford. Her husband might be underwriting the expense of the hunt, but that did not prevent them referring to her as a 'hippodrome dolly'. The men were more inclined just to admire the sight of the countess in the saddle.

Catherine did not enjoy being the butt of gossip columnists. Even worse, a London Music Hall ran for eight weeks a show in which female impersonators played the parts of the Countess and the Strumpet (the latter referring to another Quorn follower, known as Skittles, whose career echoed Catherine's own). It was all very embarrassing, and as a result Catherine refused to hunt again. In 1863 lord Stamford gave up the hunt, and Tattersalls held a sale of his hunters at Bradgate, which was attended by eight thousand people.

George-Harry now turned his attention to Newmarket, where he built up an extensive racing establishment and spent a fortune on bloodstock. Full of enthusiasm, he laid out a practice race-course around Old John, marked by stones, some of which are still present. He had another course laid out in woods at Enville, and hoped, by training his horses in such secluded locations, to steal a march on other competitors. But everything went wrong. His horses scarcely ever won a race, and before long he held an auction at Newmarket to get rid of them.

His main interest then became shooting. At Bradgate there was a good stock of pheasants, and farms

During the 19th century a Victorian gentleman of any standing collected exotic tree species and planted specimens of as many as possible on his estate. The 7th earl of Stamford planted the fine spreading cedar in the middle of this picture, along with Monkey Puzzle Trees and a number of other exotic trees throughout the Little Matlock area of the park.

Grey Family Tree: Part three – The End of the Earldom

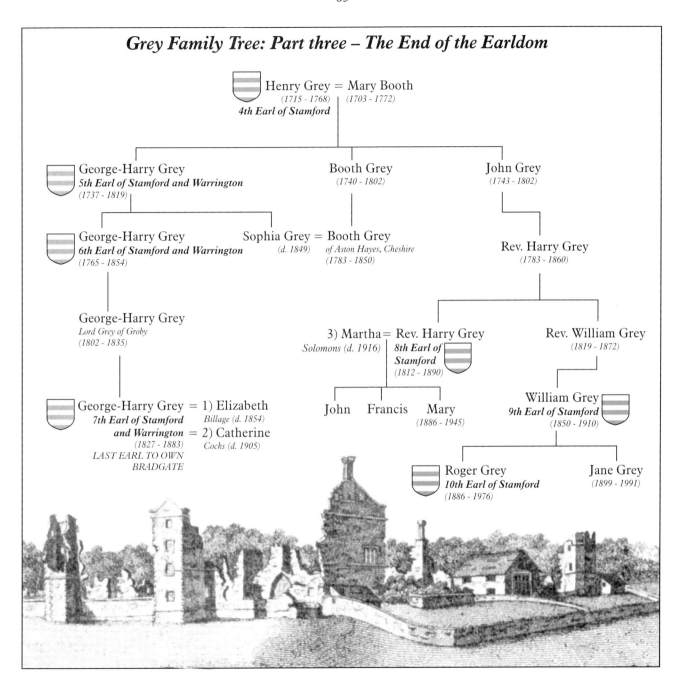

Henry Grey = Mary Booth
(1715 - 1768) | *(1703 - 1772)*
4th Earl of Stamford

George-Harry Grey
5th Earl of Stamford and Warrington
(1737 - 1819)

Booth Grey
(1740 - 1802)

John Grey
(1743 - 1802)

George-Harry Grey
6th Earl of Stamford and Warrington
(1765 - 1854)

Sophia Grey = Booth Grey
(d. 1849) | *of Aston Hayes, Cheshire*
(1783 - 1850)

Rev. Harry Grey
(1783 - 1860)

George-Harry Grey
Lord Grey of Groby
(1802 - 1835)

3) Martha = Rev. Harry Grey
Solomons (d. 1916) | **8th Earl of Stamford**
(1812 - 1890)

Rev. William Grey
(1819 - 1872)

George-Harry Grey = 1) Elizabeth
7th Earl of Stamford | *Billage (d. 1854)*
and Warrington = 2) Catherine
(1827 - 1883) | *Cocks (d. 1905)*
LAST EARL TO OWN
BRADGATE

John   Francis   Mary
(1886 - 1945)

William Grey
9th Earl of Stamford
(1850 - 1910)

Roger Grey
10th Earl of Stamford
(1886 - 1976)

Jane Grey
(1899 - 1991)

where pheasants roamed at will were charged very little rent. Great house parties, centred on the new Bradgate House, led to the slaughter of vast numbers of game birds. In January 1882 the Prince of Wales (later Edward VII) attended a shoot at Bradgate. He arrived by train at the old Midland Station in Campbell Street, Leicester, and was driven in an open carriage through streets decorated with bunting and flags. When he arrived at Bradgate House in the winter dusk the staff were lined up outside to greet him by lantern light. The following day between two and three thousand head of game were shot on Bradgate Park, and the Prince was shown round the ruins of the home of lady Jane Grey.

As the earl was also gambling, his huge fortune was dwindling. He began to mortgage property after property. As well as building Bradgate House, he also spent huge sums on Enville Hall, where the gardens and grounds vied with the greatest in the land, and a huge glass-house was erected which in size was second only to the Crystal Palace.

The winter after the Prince of Wales' visit, George-Harry took a trip to his estate at Aviemore in Scotland, where he had recently built a new wing to his hunting lodge. When he returned home ill, it was attributed to exposure to cold and damp over a long period. He died in January 1883, aged 55.

The South African Earl

As the seventh earl had not produced an heir and had no brothers, the Warrington title died out, and the eighth earl of Stamford was a distant cousin, the Rev. Harry Grey. This lord Stamford was a renegade clergyman. He was an alcoholic and his scandalous behaviour led to his family shipping him out to the Cape as a 'remittance man' (given an allowance which he could pick up from a post office as long as he stayed out of the way and stopped embarrassing them). He was not expected to succeed to the title, but due to the deaths of those with prior claims this is what happened. The Rev

Harry Grey married three times, and was rescued from the life of a down-and-out by a Cape Coloured woman called Martha Solomons, who became his third wife.

The eighth earl never returned to England, and died in 1890, leaving two surviving children by Martha Solomons: a son born before their marriage, and a daughter afterwards. Under South African law, the son became legitimate because of his parents' subsequent marriage, but it was not so in England, and a committee of the House of Lords decreed that the title should pass to the Rev Harry's cousin William.

The ninth earl of Stamford was a very different character from his predecessor, and would have made a much more suitable clergyman. Academic and worthy, he lived in London with his wife Penelope, who was a vicar's daughter, and their two children, Roger and Jane, until the death of Catherine Cocks.

Kitty Cocks, Dowager Countess

Catherine, now Dowager countess of Stamford and Warrington, had been left a life interest in all her husband's properties. She ran a profitable stud at Enville, and through her business acumen turned the estate round and made it pay again. She divided her time between Enville and Bradgate. She never lived at Dunham, where there had been trouble over the Bowdon churchwardens forbidding the ringing of the church bells on the occasion of her wedding, though she and her husband had always shown an interest in their Cheshire and Lancashire estates.

In Leicestershire she was involved in various good works, particularly the Royal Infirmary and the Institute for the Blind. Stories recalled by people with family memories of the Bradgate Estate paint a picture of a tall, elegant woman. Because of her stature, some of her occasional tables were made higher than normal. Only particularly tall and good looking footmen were employed, but attractive applicants for the position of maidservant were never engaged. In her latter years the

A 19th century engraving by an unknown artist, of Little Matlock, looking towards Newtown Linford.

staff would sometimes refer to her affectionately, but behind her back, as Old Kit.

In November 1904, winter arrived early and lady Stamford sent word to Enville Hall that the house must be kept well aired. The fires were banked up, a chimney caught light, and an inferno was soon raging through the rooms. Fire engines had difficulty traversing the snowbound lanes, and the frozen lake made water hard to obtain. The blaze got out of control, and wrought havoc on much of the great, historic house. Lady Stamford was devastated. On January 29th, 1905, she died at Bradgate House.

Cropston Reservoir

Cropston Reservoir was constructed in the mid-nineteenth century to provide the rapidly expanding town of Leicester with a reliable supply of drinking water. The site at Bradgate was one of five considered by the Leicester Water Works Company who handled the scheme and who purchased 180 acres of the Park from the earl of Stamford for £24,000. Work commenced in the late 1860s and the Reservoir was operational by May 1871. The rising waters covered the site of the old rabbit warren together with the keeper's cottage.

At full capacity the Reservoir contains 480 million gallons (about 2234 megalitres) of water which provide a surface area of 148 acres (about 59 hectares). The dam, which has a core of puddled clay, is 760 yards long, between 40 and 50 feet high and gives a depth of water of 38 feet. Whereas water from the earlier undertaking at Thornton fed water to Leicester by gravity, that from Cropston always had to be pumped. The original steam engines were taken out of commission in the 1950s and replaced by modern electrical ones. These in turn have now been updated to make use of microchip technology.

Part way through the building of the reservoir, and with costs rising, the entire operation was taken over by Leicester Corporation. The original budget was for a total of £126,000 but the final expenditure was £142,000. The cost of the dam alone accounted for £41,356 whilst the 1300 yards of wall separating the reservoir from the Park were built by George Rudkin for just 8s 10d per yard. The large labour force required was partly boarded in the homes of local people and partly housed in temporary accommodation on site. The behaviour of the men both on and off duty was strongly in the tradition of the 'navvies' who had earlier built the local canals and railways.

Cropston Reservoir is an important site for wildlife. Only twenty years after its completion, the Rev T. A. Preston had recorded 225 species of wild plants. These included the first British record for the Fleabane, *Inula britannica*. The open water provides resting and feeding for wildfowl, particularly the large numbers of ducks which over-winter here. The frequent rise and fall of the water level exposes mud which attracts wading birds on migration. Not surprisingly perhaps, the Reservoir has been declared a Site of Special Scientific Interest and is managed under a plan drawn up by the Leicestershire Wildlife Trust.

At the same time as Cropston Reservoir was constructed, a number of small pools were constructed along the River Lyn, to reduce the amount of silt and sediment flowing in to the reservoir. The result is a chain of surprisingly impressive waterfalls, which add to the scenic charm of Little Matlock.

8. THE PARTING OF THE WAYS

*I*n accordance with the seventh earl's will, on his wife's death the three main Grey estates were split up. Dunham Massey went with the title, and became the property of William, ninth earl of Stamford. When he died, in 1910, his son Roger became the tenth earl at the age of 14. Roger never married, but lived at Dunham with his mother, who died in 1959 aged 93. When Roger died in 1976, the title died out and the property passed, as arranged in his lifetime, to the National Trust. It is now open to the public during the summer months, except on Thursdays and Fridays.

Roger's younger sister, lady Jane Grey, who hated life in a stately home and longed for an ordinary house, married the local curate, Rev Peveril Turnbull, and achieved fulfilment as a country vicar's wife. In her later years she took renewed interest in her ancestry and paid several visits to Bradgate Park, inspecting it happily from the front seat of a keeper's Landrover in her late

Even while the Grey family owned Bradgate, it became a popular day-tripper's destination, and a favourite subject for early postcards such as the one below.

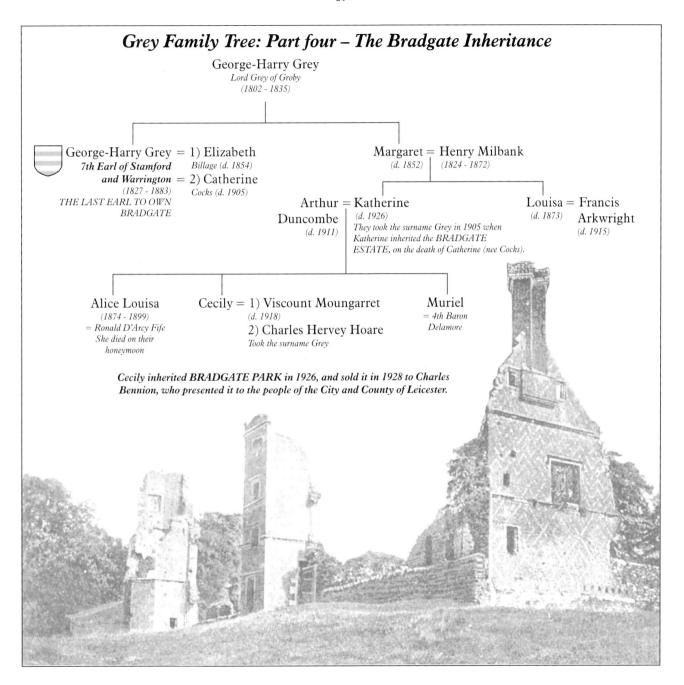

Grey Family Tree: Part four – The Bradgate Inheritance

George-Harry Grey
Lord Grey of Groby
(1802 - 1835)

George-Harry Grey
7th Earl of Stamford and Warrington
(1827 - 1883)
THE LAST EARL TO OWN BRADGATE
= 1) Elizabeth
Billage (d. 1854)
= 2) Catherine
Cocks (d. 1905)

Margaret = Henry Milbank
(d. 1852) *(1824 - 1872)*

Arthur = Katherine
Duncombe
(d. 1911)
(d. 1926)
They took the surname Grey in 1905 when Katherine inherited the BRADGATE ESTATE, on the death of Catherine (nee Cocks).

Louisa = Francis
(d. 1873) Arkwright
(d. 1915)

Alice Louisa
(1874 - 1899)
= Ronald D'Arcy Fife
She died on their honeymoon

Cecily = 1) Viscount Moungarret
(d. 1918)
2) Charles Hervey Hoare
Took the surname Grey

Muriel
= 4th Baron Delamore

*Cecily inherited **BRADGATE PARK** in 1926, and sold it in 1928 to Charles Bennion, who presented it to the people of the City and County of Leicester.*

The War Memorial, erected on the other end of the ridge occupied by Old John, commemorates the men of the Leicestershire Yeomanry who died in the Boer Wars and the two World Wars. The resulting distinctive skyline, visible from much of Leicestershire, makes the hill one of the county's most familiar landmarks.

eighties. She died in 1991, aged 92.

Enville Hall was rebuilt with money from the Insurance company, and remains a private house. George-Harry had been particularly fond of Catherine's niece, Sarah Letitia, who had been born in a Dorset workhouse, brought up in the stately home, and had married the Rev Alfred Payne, who became Rector of Enville. Under the terms of the seventh earl's will, it was Sarah Letitia's descendants who inherited the Enville estates.

The Leicestershire estates became the property of Katherine Henrietta Venezia Duncombe, daughter of George-Harry's sister Margaret. She and her husband were required to add the name of Grey to that of

Kitty Brown Remembers

My family lived in the right-hand half of what is now Marion's Cottage gift shop. There were five of us children, and I was born in 1906. In those days Bradgate Park belonged to the Grey family. Mr Haslegrave, the Agent, lived in the village, and Mr Middleton, the Keeper, lived in the Lodge in the middle of the park.

I can just remember seeing the oak trees being pollarded for what must have been the last time. I never saw the ghost of lady Jane Grey on New Year's Eve, though Mr Haslegrave was convinced he did. He went out one year specially, and said he saw her walking along by the ruins. As far as I know, she was wearing her head!

You could not wander at will over the hillsides, or up to Tyburn. You could walk along the main drive to Hallgates, but the roadway was in a poor state. Nobody bothered with it, and of course nobody had to take a car over it. You were also allowed to take a footpath from the ruins up to Old John, and there were footpaths to Anstey and Cropston, but you had to keep to the path. Lots of people came out from Leicester to walk along the main drive, but you were hardly allowed to look at the rest.

Of course, as children, we didn't always go by the rules! We loved to paddle in the brook, climb up the rocks, and play hide-and-seek in the bracken. Nobody took too much notice of what children got up to, though they would come and tell us off.

We couldn't play on the Park Field (where the car park is now) because it was boggy and smelly with sewage

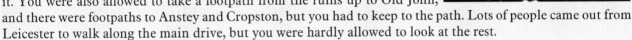

from the sewage field on Groby Lane. Sometimes we would gather mayblobs there, but had to be very careful where we put our feet.

In the Park we gathered chestnuts to eat. This was trespassing, but we always kept one person as a 'look-out' in case somebody came along and caught us. We were always in the brook, specially our family, from Marion's Cottage. We would collect frogspawn and go fishing for tiddlers, and we made a wonderful den up a tree, where the branches forked out. I was sad when that tree fell down. Four or five of us could get up at a time – girls and boys. We were great friends with the Neale children from Beech Farm – Doris, Frank, Marjorie and Wilfred. They were always the ringleaders, and somehow always got away with it. Old Glover Ball, who must have been in his 50s or 60s, proposed to Doris soon after she left school. That really was the talk of the town...

Kitty Brown (above) has lived in Newtown Linford all her life and grew up in Park Cottage (left), the right hand half of the pair of cottages now known as Marion's Cottage, the Bradgate Park shop.

Bradgate's Mystery Ditches

In the north-east corner of the Park, near the wall of the Hallgates car park, lies a remarkable series of banks and ditches, the origin and purpose of which still remain very much of a mystery. Their symmetry, size and configuration suggest strongly that they are man-made rather than natural. They begin and end for no obvious topographical reason. If they are the remains of once more extensive earthworks of a very long lost age, it is difficult to even suggest a defensive or other feature to which they might relate. The depth of the

ditches, typically eight feet, and the distances between a pair of ridges, about 24 feet, seem to rule out their use as a routeway. One idea is that they are the last remnants of a prehistoric tribal boundary similar to those known in other parts of England and possibly dating from the middle Bronze Age (around 1400 BC). It has even been suggested that they were constructed for training recruits in the techniques of trench warfare during World War One.

Duncombe. She put the estate up for sale in the 1920s, and Bradgate Park was bought by a local industrialist, Mr Charles Bennion, in 1928, after Katherine's death, from her daughter Cecily. Mr Bennion, of the British United Shoe Machinery Company, presented it to the city and county of Leicester 'to be preserved in its natural state for the quiet enjoyment of the people of Leicestershire', available for all time as a place of recreation. It has been administered since then by the Bradgate Park Trust.

The popular perception of Bradgate Park as a place where time has stood still, is due in large measure to the abandonment of the house and the fact that it escaped the attentions of the landscape gardeners of the eighteenth century. At their other two properties, the Greys were in the forefront of new fashions of landscape design. They created avenues and then destroyed them, excavated lakes, moved earth and constructed cascades and ornamental buildings. What the Greys did introduce to Bradgate were some exotic imported trees. These have caused some controversy, but for most people the mature Cedars of Lebanon and Monkey

Above: Charles Bennion, benefactor.
Below left: The wishing stone, in Little Matlock.

Puzzles in Little Matlock are part of the wonderful variety of nature, to be mourned when a gale brings another of them down.

Because of Bradgate Park, most Leicestershire people are as familiar with deer and bracken and hills and rocks as if they lived in the Highlands of Scotland. The scale of the land is intimate, but it is unrivalled as a place of blissful memories. A Leicestershire exile in the tropics dreams of Bradgate in the snow, while the winter-bound city dweller plans a trip to Bradgate in the spring. Countless marriages have been proposed there. The Greys owned it for five hundred years. Now it belongs to the people for all time.

Bradgate Park as a Site of Special Scientific Interest (SSSI)

The park is important not only on account of its spectacular scenery and strong historical connections but also because it has a rich and varied flora and fauna together with marked geological interests. Bradgate is one of the finest examples of ancient parkland in Leicestershire. The large areas of open ground have species typical of the moorlands of Southern England yet still support some of the rarer ones for which Charnwood was once well known. Some of the plants demonstrate the area's likenesses with two other outstanding places in the midlands: Sherwood Forest and Cannock Chase. Bradgate also contains some of the last fragments of wet heath in the county, with such species as Dyer's Greenweed, Common Milkwort, Crossleaved Heath and Mountain fern. In addition, the margins of Cropston Reservoir support nationally scarce species such as Orange foxtail Grass, Needle spike-rush, small water-pepper and Golden Dock. The marshy ground of the north and east of the Park, dominated by purple moor grass, has a number of locally rare plants – for example, moonwort, Creeping Willow and Lesser Skulcap. Small pools contain Bogmoss and are inhabited by the broad-bodied chaser dragonfly and two species of Hydroporus water beetle, both rare in Leicestershire.

Yet another outstanding feature of the Park is the richness of the invertebrate fauna, which is a reflection of the diversity of different habitats in the park and is especially related to the ancient oaks. These produce in particular an abundance of rotting wood which is a habitat seldom found in woodlands under modern

commercial management elsewhere. The ancient trees present a continuity reaching back over five hundred years and more. Some of the creatures they support suggest unbroken links with the wildwood of pre-history. Over six hundred species of beetles for example, and many unusual and uncommon spiders have been been found present.

The park supports a good variety of breeding birds including woodcock, sparrowhawk, three species of woodpecker and whinchat. Even more important are the populations of species declining in Leicestershire such as Barn owl and redstart. The totals recorded for the park are greatly increased if the resident and visiting water fowl and other birds of Cropston Reservior are taken into account.

The British mammal fauna is well represented too, particularly by the deer population, members of which are probably descended from those first introduced to the park in the thirteenth century. (See page 56). Several kinds of reptiles, too, are present, such as slow worm, adder and common lizard, all species struggling to survive in other parts of Leicestershire.

The rocks of Bradgate (see page 8) have been recognised as of national importance for what they tell us about events in pre-Cambrian times, approximately six hundred million years ago. Certain of these rocks contain some of the oldest known fossils including the famous *Charnia masoni*.

Bradgate Park was recognised at an early date as a very special place and was notified as a Site of Special Scientific Interest under the terms of the National Parks and Access to the Countryside Act of 1949. This status was later confirmed by section 28 of the Wildlife and Countryside Act of 1981. Although thus protected in principle by statute, Bradgate shares the same uncertainties and pressures faced by many similarly designated areas. Its survival as a haven for such a diverse range of plants and animals requires the on-going commitment of the visitors, staff and Bradgate Park Trustees.

9. A Self-Guided Walk Through Bradgate Park

*T*his short walk through the 'Low Park' is about 1¾ miles (2.8km) from end to end. It points out some of the features of historic interest that can be seen without leaving the tarmac drive. Features 9, 19 and 20 may take a little searching for when the bracken is high in the summer. There is much to commend this walk for a fine winter's day.

1 Coppiced Oak Tree: Four trees appear to grow from one stump. Coppicing, cutting a tree near the ground, produces shoots which develop into poles. Every 7 to 20 years they would be harvested. These specimens haven't been cut for over 80 years

2 Little Matlock: A steep-sided wooded valley named after the rugged scenery of Matlock in Derbyshire.

3 Monkey Puzzle Tree and Cedar of Lebanon: Introduced into the Park in the nineteenth century, when it was fashionable to plant exotic species in a country estate. Look around for other specimens in this area.

4 Pools and Waterfalls: These were created at the same time as the reservoir. The waterfalls aerate the water, and the pools, which contain fish such as trout, crayfish, and stickleback, allow silt to be deposited before reaching the reservoir.

5 Wishing Stone: This marks the site of a dam across the Lyn, which created a head of water to feed the leat.

6 Leat: A channel designed to take water from the River Lyn to the House. The construction of this feature was a fine piece of engineering of the early 16th C.

7 Line of the Park Pale: Here the line of the perimeter pale (bank and ditch) of the first Bradgate Park is crossed. It shows as a long shallow depression where the grass is green even in the driest summer. It is continued on the far side of the stream and runs uphill through the deer sanctuary. (see pages 14-16)

8 Bennion Plaque: A plaque to Charles Bennion who bought the Park from the Greys, and gave it 'for the quiet enjoyment of the people of Leicestershire'.

9 Moated site: The site of the lodge of the keepers of the first Bradgate Park. The lodge became redundant when Thomas Grey laid out his 'new' park in c. 1500.

10 Pheasantry: This large rectangular enclosure with high stone walls was built to keep predators away from newly hatched game birds.

11 Grey Plaque: A small notice recounting the death of Roger Grey, tenth earl of Stamford, whose ancestors owned the Park for five centuries. The title is now extinct.

12 Bridge over the Lyn: Important visitors approaching the House from Leicester used to cross the river here. King William did so on his visit to Bradgate in 1696.

13 Bradgate House Ruins : see pages 22-26. The Chapel is the only roofed building in the ruins, and contains the fine alabaster tomb of Henry Grey, who was created baron Groby, and who died in 1614.

Peacocks now inhabit the ruins and have startled many visitors (and perhaps fuelled a few rumours of ghosts) with their blood curdling calls.

14 Site of Watermill: powered by water which was carried along the leat.

15 Sluice Channel

16 Water Meadow: The water meadow is an area of flat land created in the nineteenth century to improve the Park's grazing. Water for flooding was led from the Lyn along the channels (which run alongside the tarmac drive) and into brick-lined conduits. The sluices, now gone, regulated the flow, direction and depth of water in the conduits.

Red deer roam widely around the park, but are most often seen in the areas near the ruins and water meadow.

17 Keeper's Lodge: Built at the end of the nineteenth century to replace the one lost to the reservoir (see p. 52).

18 Deer Barn, Visitor Centre and Toilets.

19 Line of the Park Pale: This shows as a bank and ditch emerging from Coppice Plantation, crossing the tarmac drive and then disappearing under the water of the reservoir. (see map on page 10).

20 Ridge and Furrow. This characteristic feature of medieval cultivation is part of the ploughland of the lost village of Bradgate. (see page 14). It was incorporated into his 'new' park by Thomas Grey in around 1500.

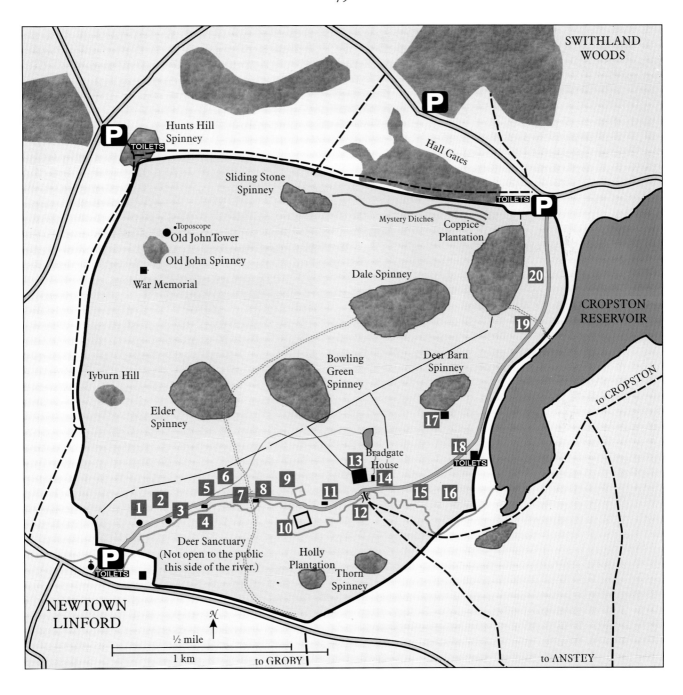

SWITHLAND WOODS

P

Hunts Hill
Spinney

P
TOILETS

Hall Gates

Sliding Stone
Spinney

TOILETS
P

Mystery Ditches   Coppice
Plantation

•Toposcope
●Old John Tower

Old John Spinney

Dale Spinney

20

■ War Memorial

19

CROPSTON
RESERVOIR

Bowling
Green
Spinney

Deer Barn
Spinney

Tyburn Hill

17 ■

to CROPSTON

Elder
Spinney

18
TOILETS

6

13   Bradgate
House
9   14

5

11

15   16

1   2

7   8

3

12

4

10

P
TOILETS

Deer Sanctuary
(Not open to the public
this side of the river.)

Holly
Plantation

Thorn
Spinney

NEWTOWN
LINFORD

N

½ mile

1 km

to GROBY

to ANSTEY

A Hill Walk

Hunt's Hill (Old John Car Park) to Newtown Linford — 1¼ miles (2km).

Between the Car Park and the Park proper is Hunt's Hill, a wooded area outside the boundary wall. It was a prehistoric meeting place at the crossing of ancient tracks.

Once inside the park there is a short but steep climb from the entrance gate to the summit of Old John, offering panoramic views over the surrounding countryside. The toposcope, which indicates the direction and distance of other landmarks in the area, was purchased by the villagers of Newtown Linford from the proceeds of their 1953 pageant.

Just beyond Old John Tower (for which see pages 52 and 55) is a curious brick and rock wall. This is all that remains of the stables built to accommodate the seventh earl of Stamford's race horses, which once exercised on a course around Old John.

Beside the stables, pass through one of the entrances into Old John Spinney. There are several walled spinneys in the park, but this is the only one the public is permitted to enter. They were walled (to keep out the deer) and planted in the eighteenth century to provide game coverts. Beaters would drive the birds out of a wooded hilltop covert, forcing them to fly across the valley towards the safety of a neighbouring spinney — directly over the waiting guns of the shooting party.

After passing through the spinney, the next summit is the site of the War Memorial, dedicated to the men of the Leicestershire Yeomanry who lost their lives in the Boer Wars, and the Two World Wars.

Continuing south, a broad grassy path leads down a steep slope past the crags of the slate agglomerates (see pages 8-9). A path leads to a lower hilltop spinney — without a wall — known as Tyburn. This is named after Tyburn Hill in London, the site of public executions until 1783. The Bradgate Tyburn was apparently used not as a place to hang criminals but somewhere to castrate young hunting dogs, at a distance from the kennels, so that their yelps would not be heard by the other hounds.

There is a choice of paths down to the dividing wall between the High and Low Parks. A gap at the end of this wall leads to the Newtown Linford entrance.

The course of this walk can be seen on the aerial photograph on page 6, running from the bottom right hand corner of the picture to the top centre.

A Circular Route

The Hill Walk ends where the Self-Guided Walk on page 77 starts. The two routes can be joined together and followed to Hallgates. Then, continuing in an anti-clockwise direction, follow the path alongside the boundary wall, past the 'Mystery Ditches' (see page 72), up the hill and back to the Old John car park. This provides a walk of some 4½ miles (7 km).

Visitors are, of course, at liberty to wander anywhere they wish in the park, except for the designated deer reserve beyond the river, and the walled spinneys. The ruins are open at specified times in the summer months.

Further Reading

AIRS, Malcolm. *The Tudor and Jacobean Country House, A Building History.* Alan Sutton Publishing (1995)

CANTOR, Leonard. *The Medieval Parks of England: A Gazeteer.* Loughborough University (1983)

CANTOR, Leonard and SQUIRES, Anthony. *The Historic Parks and Gardens of Leicestershire and Rutland.* Kairos Press (1997)

CHAPMAN, Hester. *Lady Jane Grey.* Jonathon Cape (1962)

CROCKER, J (Ed.) *Charnwood Forest, A Changing Landscape.* Sycamore Press/Loughborough Naturalists' Club (1981)

DAVEY, R. P. B. *Lady Jane Grey, the Nine Days Queen and Her Times.* Methuen (1909)

FORSYTH, Marie. *The History of Bradgate.* Bradgate Park Trust (1974)

FORD, Trevor D. *The Rocks of Bradgate.* Bradgate Park Trust (1974)

LUKE, Mary. *The Nine Days Queen.* William Morrow & Co. New York (1986)

MATHEW, David. *Lady Jane Grey, The Setting of the Reign.* Eyre Methuen (1972)

McWHIRR, Alan. Brickmaking in Leicestershire before about 1710. *Trans. Leics Arch & Hist Soc.* Vol 71. (1997) pp.37-59

OTTER, Jack. *The Birds of Bradgate.* Bradgate Park Trust (1976)

PLOWDEN, Alison. *Lady Jane Grey and the House of Suffolk.* Sidgwick & Jackson (1985)

RAMSEY, D. A. *A Time Line to Old John.* Volcano Publishing (1996)

RAMSEY, D. A. *Break Fast at Bradgate.* Volcano Publishing (1996);

RAMSEY, D. A. *Was there a Village Called Bradgate?* David Ramsey (1998)

SQUIRES, A. E. & HUMPHREY, W. *The Medieval Parks of Charnwood Forest.* Sycamore Press (1986)

SQUIRES, Anthony. *Leicestershire and Rutland Woodlands Past and Present.* Kairos Press (1994)

SQUIRES, Anthony. *Donington Park and the Hastings Connection.* Kairos Press (1996)

STEVENSON, Joan. *The Greys of Bradgate.* Bradgate Park Trust (1974)

STEVENSON, Joan. *A Family Guide to Bradgate Park and Swithland Woods.* Sycamore Press (1979)

STEVENSON, Joan. *A Family Guide to Charnwood Forest.* Sycamore Press (1982), now available from Kairos Press.

STEVENSON, Joan. *Country House Parks of Leicestershire.* (Sycamore Leaves series) Sycamore Press (1985)

STEVENSON, Joan (ed.). *Memories of Newtown Linford and Bradgate House.* Kairos Press (1994)

STEVENSON, Joan. *Newtown Linford, The Old Buildings and their Occupants.* Kairos Press (1998)

WEBSTER, Michael. *Birds of Charnwood.* Kairos Press (1997)

The birdlife of Bradgate Park and Cropston Reservoir can also be traced from the Annual Reports of the Loughborough Naturalists' Club and Bulletins of the Leicestershire and Rutland Ornithological Society.

Acknowledgements

The authors wish to record their appreciation to the many people who have shared with them their knowledge of Bradgate Park and the Grey family. Some, like Edward Turner, Sir Andrew Martin, Edward Stewart Gray and lady Jane Turnbull, are sadly no longer with us. We are grateful to the staff of the National Trust at Dunham Massey; Clive Alford; M. J. Scott-Bolton and Mrs Sandy Haynes at Enville; Michael Harrison and the Bradgate Park staff and Trust; Leicestershire Record Office; Peter Lee, David Ramsey, Margaret Pratt, and David Smith who also drew our attention to the earlier work of D A (Peter) Blakesley.

With this book specifically in mind we wish to express our thanks to Brian Anderson, Kitty Brown, R and K Burrows, John Crocker, Joy Geary, Colin Green, Alan Hamilton, Robert F Hartley, Michael Jeeves, Piers Keating, Ralph Leek, Leicestershire Museums Service, Peter Liddle, David Lyne, Mervyn Stevenson, Michael Webster, Gill Weightman and all those other people who have contributed in one way or another. In particular we owe a great deal to the zeal and technological expertise of our publisher, Robin Stevenson of Kairos Press.

Index

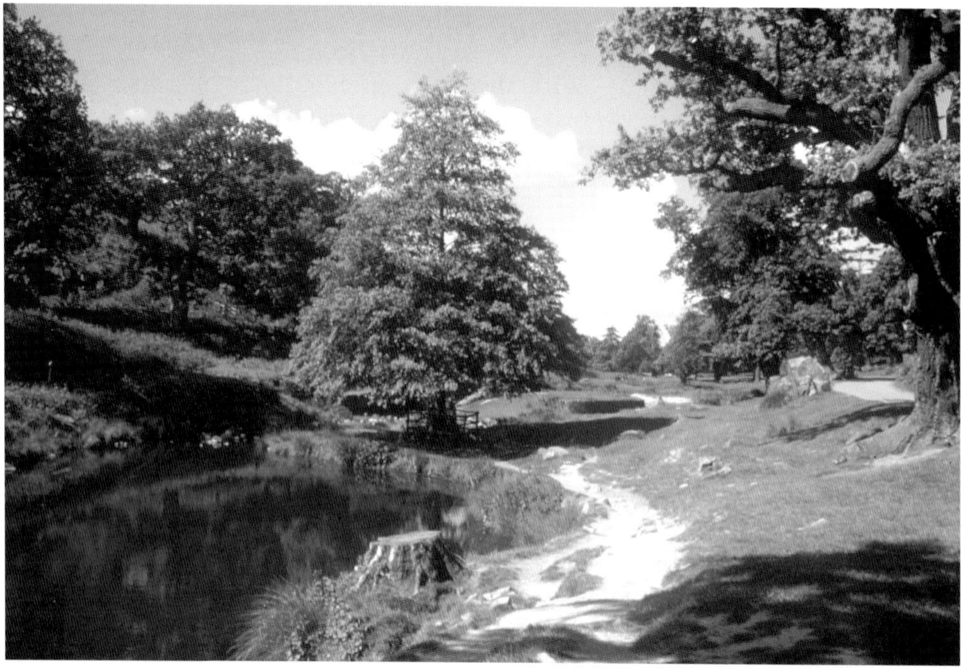